BANCASSURANCE IN EUROPE

Also by Tobias C. Hoschka

CROSS-BORDER ENTRY IN EUROPEAN
RETAIL FINANCIAL SERVICES

Bancassurance in Europe

Tobias C. Hoschka
E. C. Research Fellow
University of Oxford

St. Martin's Press

First published in Great Britain 1994 by
THE MACMILLAN PRESS LTD
Houndmills, Basingstoke, Hampshire RG21 2XS
and London
Companies and representatives
throughout the world

A catalogue record for this book is available
from the British Library.

ISBN 0-333-62814-4

Printed in Great Britain by
Antony Rowe Ltd
Chippenham, Wiltshire

First published in the United States of America 1994 by
Scholarly and Reference Division,
ST. MARTIN'S PRESS, INC.,
175 Fifth Avenue,
New York, N.Y. 10010

ISBN 0-312-12278-0

Library of Congress Cataloging-in-Publication Data applied for

Contents

Acknowledgements

Undertaking research is never done without the help of others. I would therefore like to thank particularly Bimal Prodhan for many helpful comments and suggestions which have significantly improved this study. I am also very grateful to Ian Kessler and Keith Blois as well as Jacques Girin and Alain Jeunemaitre of the Centre de Recherche en Gestion at Ecole Polytechnique in Paris for hosting me as a visiting scholar and following my research with much interest. Finally, I would like to express my thanks to my editor at Macmillan, Giovanna Davitti, for her comments and assisitance which ensured the successful completion of this book.

As part of the study, a range of personal interviews with firm officials was undertaken. These interviews informed both the general sections as well as forming the basis for the case studies. I am therefore very grateful to all those individuals who took the time to participate in the interviews and were helpful in the collection of data and information.

List of Tables

List of Figures

Introduction

Motivation and objectives of the study

One of the most significant developments in European financial services over the past years has been the increasing convergence of banking and insurance in the retail area. This trend towards *bancassurance* or *Allfinanz* refers primarily to banks entering the insurance sector by offering insurance products to their retail customers. While the first ventures into bancassurance in Europe occurred as early as the late 1960s when TSB, Lloyds and Barclays entered the life insurance sector, it was not until the mid-1980s that a large number of European banks started entering insurance on a broader scale. Frequently cited success stories include Crédit Agricole's de novo start-up, Prédica, which quickly achieved a leading position in the French market, or TSB in the UK which derives 30 percent of its profits in retail financial services from insurance. These examples have inspired many European bankers to attempt emulating these successful ventures by also entering the insurance sector. By 1993, more than half of the large European banks have incorporated insurance products into their product portfolios. As a result, the former cosy co-existence of the banking and insurance industries has turned into direct competition in the financial services market. Today, cross-industry penetration has already reached a stage where analysts increasingly speak of a 'retail financial services industry' rather than referring to retail banking and insurance as separate and distinct sectors.

Entry activities of banks into insurance were induced by a variety of factors including a more liberal regulatory regime permitting banks and insurers to cross formerly strictly-defined boundaries, the increased share of life insurance products in total savings threatening banks' deposit retail base, and dwindling margins in banks' traditional business lines forcing them to look for new high-return, low-risk business opportunities.

The success of banks 'stealing away' business from insurers differs between the life and non-life sectors as well as between European countries, however. Figure 1 shows the market share of different distribution channels for life insurance in 1992. Banks play the most important role in life insurance distribution in France and Spain, while having lower market shares in Germany and Belgium. Over the past decade they have been able to increase their share significantly in all countries, however. In France, for example, banks accounted for 22 per cent of life insurance distribution in 1984, while by 1992 this figure had risen to more than 40 per cent. In general insurance, however, inroads of banks into insurance have been less significant with a much lower bank share of distribution varying between 2 per cent in France and 5 per cent in Britain.[1]

Figure 1: Market share of different distribution channels in life insurance in 1992 in 7 EC countries

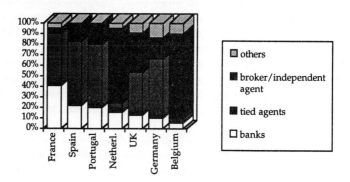

Source: own collection from Swiss Reinsurance/Sigma; 2/1992; *The Economist*, May 8th, 1993, p.107 and national statistics.

A range of issues arise in the context of banks' entry into insurance. For example, what industry- and firm-level factors explain the dramatic increase in banks' market share in life insurance distribution in some countries? Is it possible to identify certain entry strategies which promise the greatest success for banks? And how does the choice of the entry vehicle affect the outcome of the venture into insurance?

The literature addressing these and other issues in the context of bancassurance has been scarce, so far. In particular, the risks and potential pay-offs for a bank entering the insurance sector are not well-understood. While there have been a number of descriptive studies dealing with industry dynamics and specific experiences of individual banks, a comprehensive analytical approach to both theoretical and empirical factors is not available.

This study aims to close this gap in the literature by providing a thorough analysis of the whole range of theoretical and practical issues linked to the phenomenon of banks' entry into insurance. Two main areas require scrutiny in this context.

First, the issue *why* banks enter insurance needs to be discussed. This requires analysis of industry-level factors including regulatory changes and industry dynamics which impact the competitive environment of banks. Concerning industry-level factors, for example, how do recent changes in the regulatory framework of financial services influence the trend towards bancassurance? And what industry-level incentives exist for banks to enter the insurance market? How do demographic changes, tax considerations, economic trends, insurance penetration, saturation levels and savings trends influence banks' incentives to enter insurance? Concerning firm-level incentives, on the other hand, how significant is the synergy potential between banking and insurance and how can such effects best be exploited?

Second, the issue *how* banks enter insurance requires scrutiny. Four alternative entry routes can be distinguished: de novo entry, a co-operative distribution alliance with an insurer, a joint venture, and a merger or an acquisition. Relative advantages and disadvantages of each entry route need to be analysed, based on both theoretical considerations and a comprehensive analysis of available empirical evidence. For example, does de novo entry leave a greater choice of product design and distribution methods and therefore offer greater scope for designing a tailored entry strategy than other entry vehicles? Do mergers and acquisitions pose insurmountable problems of aligning two possibly very different corporate and selling cultures or are there successful approaches for integration? Do strategic distribution alliances offer much in terms of profit potential for the involved bank and insurer or are they doomed to failure due to problems of incentive incompatibilities? Finally, do joint ventures provide a way of pooling complementary resources and accumulated know-how or are there similar cultural compatibility problems as for mergers and acquisitions?

The emphasis of the analysis is placed on the issue whether it is possible to identify systematic trends and characteristics for different entry vehicles and why it is that some banks have been extremely successful, whereas others are still struggling with their entry strategy into insurance.

Structure of the Study

Chapter one of the study addresses the question *why* banks enter insurance and have chosen in particular the life insurance sector. The analysis differentiates between industry- and firm-level factors. Concerning industry-level factors the first section analyses regulatory and legislative changes and provides a brief discussion of industry dynamics in the banking sector. In addition, it presents a detailed analysis of economic incentives for banks to enter the life insurance sector and analyses an aggregate database of insurance entry activities of the largest 60 EC banks.

Concerning firm-level factors part one focuses on the synergy explanation of entry activities, providing a definition and analysing the significance of scale and scope economies for the case of bancassurance. In addition, it provides a discussion of the limits of synergy and analyses some organizational issues in this context.

The second chapter of the study focuses on the issue of *how* banks enter the insurance sector. It analyses thirteen case studies of banks' entry activities into insurance representing the most important and most frequently cited examples in Europe. It analyses publicly available information derived from a number of sources such as industry reports, press clippings and annual reports and supplements these by corporate-level interviews aimed at gaining a better insight into underlying firm strategies and pinning down the critical success factors. The section also provides a comparative analysis of the four different entry vehicles, focusing on the question whether any one vehicle appears more successful than its strategic alternatives. In addition, it focuses on the key success factors in the context of banks' entry into insurance including successful market segmentation and distribution as well as the issue of combining the salary system of banking with the commission-based approach of insurance.

A summary and an outlook of the implications for banks' strategies conclude the study.

---

1 See *The Economist*, May 8th, 1993, p.107.

Chapter One:
Why do Banks enter Insurance?
Industry- and Firm-level Incentives

This first chapter of the study deals with the economic incentives for a bank to enter the insurance sector, both from an industry- as well as a firm-level perspective. It addresses the following key issues:
- How has the regulatory environment changed over the past decade and facilitated the crossing of formerly strictly defined industry boundaries between banking and insurance?
- How has the general operating environment of banking changed and influenced the background against which banks decide to enter insurance?
- What is the growth and profit potential of life insurance and what role does it play in the EC countries?
- What firm-level factors influence banks' decision to enter insurance and in particular what synergy effects exist between banking and insurance?

Section one addresses changes in the regulatory environment, since these are crucial for understanding entry activities in different countries. The second section then analyses industry dynamics in the banking sector, while presenting aggregate data on entry movements of banks into insurance in section 3. The fourth section examines *industry*-level incentives for banks to enter life insurance, whereas the fifth section focuses on *firm*-level reasons. It thereby focuses on a synergy effects explanation of cross-industry penetration and provides an analysis of the significance of size economies in financial services.

1. Bancassurance: the regulatory environment

In most countries, regulators have for a long time strictly enforced the *principle of separation* between banking and insurance

business. It was only most recently that regulators have started
to relax strict restrictions on banks and insurers to enter each
other's traditional lines of business.[1] This section analyses the
current regulatory environment in the EC countries, Japan and
the US in greater detail, as well critically discussing the reasons
which are usually cited for the regulatory principle of separation.

In general, regulations concerning cross-industry penetration
in financial services can be divided into three groups: regulations
concerning production, distribution of products and ownership
of a bank or an insurer respectively.

The first group of regulations concerns the production of insurance by banks and of banking services by insurers which is
generally prohibited in almost all countries. A recent study by
the OECD (1992) which surveys reasons for such restrictions
lists three major arguments. Firstly, insurance products are
claimed to be 'inherently' different from banking products requiring a different level of expertise and know-how which
banks supposedly do not possess. Secondly, risk factors are different in insurance and banking. Thirdly, tie-in sales such as
linking a mortgage to a life policy, for example, may convey
market power to the supplier if the consumer can only purchase
the combined product and conditions for the two products cannot be individually assessed. None of these arguments appear
convincing, however.

Consider first the argument that banking and insurance
products are 'inherently' different. In order to overcome entry
barriers resulting from lack of know-how and experience, both
banks and insurers could either 'buy in' executives and personnel with the desired expertise, enter a strategic alliance or a joint
venture or simply acquire a bank or an insurer, respectively.
Thus, lack of industry or operational know-how does not appear to constitute a legitimate reason for restricting cross-industry entry in an economic environment where labour has become
increasingly mobile across industries and required expertise can
be acquired through market transactions.

Secondly, the fact that risk in banking and insurance are of a
different nature and not necessarily correlated is more likely to
contribute to the stability of the financial services firm rather
than constituting an argument to restrict cross-industry entry,
as diversification reduces overall risk at constant return. As the
standard results of portfolio theory demonstrate (e.g.

Markowitz, 1959; Copeland and Weston, 1988), risks which have a low correlation factor are likely to lead to a more stable flow of returns, thus reducing overall operating risk of the diversified firm. This results from the fact that when one line of business faces a slump, negative results in this division may be compensated by a surplus in another division operating in a more favourable environment.

Thirdly, tie-in sales of banking and insurance products may be regulated on specific terms by ensuring transparency as well as the possibility to purchase both products separately as well as jointly. Such regulations can be easily incorporated into existing competition law provisions.

In summary, it becomes apparent that traditional arguments for the regulatory principle of separating production of banking and insurance do not hold when subjected to closer scrutiny.

The most compelling argument for separating production of services between the two sectors not mentioned in the OECD study, is the danger that banks may be tempted to use long-term assets from their insurance division to fulfill short-term liabilities in their banking division in the case of liquidity needs. Similar to companies which embezzle funds from pension funds in case of dire liquidity needs, banks may be tempted to use long-term insurance funds to satisfy short-term capital needs. While such practice should be generally prohibited, supervisors may find it hard to enforce such separation of funds in particular when there is no strict legal segregation of capital and firms employ 'creative accounting' to hide their activities. This argument, which is also the main justification for separating production of life and non-life insurance, loses force when there is strict separation between banking and insurance subsidiaries in a holding company or if banks merely distribute and do not underwrite insurance products. In practice, regulators have therefore found it preferable to allow banks and insurers to engage in distribution activities or to maintain separate legal entities when pursuing cross-industry entry activities, rather than producing services in-house. As a result, the survey of regulatory provisions by the OECD (1992) shows that in all 12 EC countries as well as in Japan and the US both banks and insurers are prohibited to engage in production of insurance and banking services respectively.

Table 1.1: Regulations concerning distribution of insurance and banking products in the EC, Japan and the US

	Distribution	
	by a bank of an insurance product	by an insurer of a bank product
Belgium	A	F*
Denmark	A	A
France	A	L
Germany	A	F*
Greece	L	F*
Ireland	A	F*
Italy	A	F*
Luxemb.	L	F*
Netherl.	A	F*
Portugal	L	F*
Spain	L	F*
UK	A	L
Japan	F	L
US	L	F*

Notes: F = Forbidden, F* = Forbidden in principle except when products are connex to insurance activity, E = Exceptional, L = Limited.

Source: OECD (1992).

The second main group of regulations concerns that of distribution of banking and insurance services. Table 1.1 shows that in most surveyed countries banks are given a greater degree of freedom of distribution than insurers. However, specific regulations vary significantly between individual countries, (OECD, 1992, p. 23-27). In Portugal, for example, distribution of insurance products is permitted on the condition that no advisory functions are undertaken. In France, banks were given the authority to distribute insurance products by the 1984 Banking Act provided that bank employees are qualified as authorised insurance agents. In Greece distribution is only permitted in towns with less than 10,000 inhabitants. Similarly, in the US federally-chartered banks can only distribute products in towns with less than 5,000 inhabitants.[2] In the UK the 1986 Financial Services Act allows for insurance product distribution of banks if the banker acts as an independent broker or distributes the products of only one insurer. Finally, in Japan banks are allowed to distribute insurance products through subsidiaries which act as independent intermediaries.

Concerning distribution of banking products by insurers, restrictions are greater than for banks. A number of EC countries interpret the first EC directives on non-life (1973) and life (1973) insurance as principally prohibiting the distribution of banking products by insurers. The vast majority of countries therefore do not allow the distribution of banking products except for those products which are directly related to the insurance sector. Such products include, for example, insurance policies with a savings or investment component, or pension products. Strict restrictions on the distribution of bank products have recently been reduced in some countries including Denmark, France and the UK on grounds of creating a more level playing field between banks and insurers, since there is no immediate regulatory reason for allowing banks to distribute insurance products but not permitting insurers to distribute banking products.

The third main group of regulations concerns entry into insurance or banking through de novo entry or acquisition of an equity stake. Table 1.2 shows regulations concerning these entry modes.

Concerning creation of de novo subsidiaries, most countries permit such entry moves. In the banking sector exceptions among the EC countries are Belgium where some banks have nevertheless set up insurance entitites with the permission of the Banking Commission and France where there are some limitations on banks owning insurance subsidiaries. In the UK building societies are only permitted to own life insurance subsidiaries, while the Bank of England does not allow banks to have civil liability subsidiaries. Japan generally prohibits banks owning insurance subsidiaries, while the US imposes severe restrictions (OECD, 1992, p. 27-30).

For insurance companies owning banking subsidiaries there are restrictions in France and the Netherlands, while such ownership is principally prohibited in Japan and the US.

Regulations concerning equity participations in banks and insurers respectively are more varied. While there are strict limitations in Japan, the US and Belgium, there are some limitations in France and the Netherlands. Restrictions on equity participations in banks by insurers exist in about half the countries surveyed. In general, equity participations, in particular when reaching a majority stake, not only require approval by the banking and insurance regulators but also by the competition policy authorities which scrutinise mergers and acquisitions according to their compatibility with ensuring effective competition and preventing market power.

Table 1.2: Regulations concerning start-up and ownership of insurance products in the EC, Japan and the US

	Start up of		Equity Stake	
	an insurance subsidiary by a bank	a banking subsidiary by an insurer	of a bank in an insurance company	of an insurance company in a bank
Belgium	SL	A	SL	A
Denmark	A	A	A	A
France	L	L	L	L
Germany	A	A/L	A	L
Greece	A	A	A	L
Ireland	A	A	A	L
Italy	A	A	A	A
Luxemb.	A	A	A	A
Netherl.	A	L	L	L
Portugal	A	A	A	L
Spain	A	A	A	A
UK	A	A	A	A
Japan	F	F	SL	SL
US	SL	SL	SL	SL

Notes: A = Allowed, F = Forbidden, L = Limited, SL = Strictly Limited

Source: OECD (1992).

In summary, entry into insurance by banks is subject to significant regulatory restrictions. This is in stark contrast to other industries where cross-industry penetration is viewed neutrally by the regulatory authorities. In fact, from an economic policy point of view, cross-industry entry is usually encouraged, as it is likely to lead to greater competition among firms with accompanying pressure on prices and margins resulting in increased consumer surplus. Regulators in financial services have recognised these potential benefits and in some countries they have therefore responded by facilitating cross-industry entry between banks and insurers.

At the same time, however, it was and still is frequently argued in financial services that competition may have detrimental effects on economic welfare and can even be "excessive" (e.g. Vives, 1991). This view results from the argument that failures of financial services firms may lead to contagious runs on financial institutions and threaten public confidence in the stability of the financial system as a whole. Thus, unlike in the industrial sector, firm failures in financial services are not considered to be part of the system-inherent process of 'weeding out' non-competitive firms in a market economy, but are events which are to be prevented. This argument loses force, however, if adequate safety mechanisms exist in order to reduce such runs. These include lender of last resort facilities of the central bank as well as deposit insurance schemes. Lender of last resort facilities refer to stand-by financing by the central bank for commercial banks facing liquidity crises (Bagehot, 1873; Humphrey, 1989; Kindleberger; 1978). Deposit insurance schemes, on the other hand, refer to financial protection of deposits of retail customer in case of bank insolvency.[3] As a result of these safety mechanisms, regulators have increasingly departed from their traditional stance of directly interfering in the banking sector and have instead adopted a more restrained approach allowing greater competition between financial institutions (e.g. Brittan, 1991). One result of such a more restrained regulatory approach is the abolition of several regulations concerning cross-industry penetration between banking and insurance. Thus, while there are still a number of regulatory restrictions concerning cross-industry penetration, it is likely that such entry barriers will be further reduced in the future, as regulators realise the potential welfare benefits of increasing competition in the financial services sector.

The next section proceeds to analyse the state of the European banking industry which is significant to understand the background against which banks form the decision to enter insurance.

2. The state of the European banking industry

European banking has been subject to a significant degree of change over the past decade. Regulatory reform and liberalisation, increased competition caused by excess capacity as well as new entry and technological progress especially in the area of information systems have led to ever-increasing demands on man-

agement and have posed unparalleled challenges for the strategic steering of banks (e.g. Gardener, 1991). This section gives a
brief overview of the main factors of change which have impacted the banking industry and which constitute the background against which banks decide to enter a new line of business such as insurance.

Banking has traditionally been an industry characterised by a
high degree of public regulation. Such regulatory intervention is
commonly justified by two economic arguments: firstly, the nature of financial products is such that they are highly complex
and product qualities may be discovered only ex post (e.g.
Nelson, 1970; Darby and Karni, 1973; Shapiro, 1983). As a result,
asymmetric information between service providers and consumers ensues which may lead to problems of moral hazard
(Stiglitz and Weis, 1981; Stiglitz and Arnott, 1990) and is frequently cited as justifying regulatory intervention on grounds of
consumer protection.

The second major reason for regulating financial services is
the need to secure systemic stability and prevent contagious
runs on financial institutions (Diamond and Dybvig, 1983;
Postlewaite and Vives, 1987; Jacklin and Battacharya, 1988;
Kaufman, 1988). As argued above, regulators have increasingly
realised, however, that in order to achieve this policy objective it
is not necessary to rely on direct interference such as fixing interest rates or commissions but that it is possible to achieve financial stability by ensuring that capital bases are sound and
that adequate emergency means such as lender of last resort
facilities and deposit insurance are in place if an insolvency occurs.[4]

While the deterring example of the Savings & Loans crisis in
the US (e.g. White, 1989; Kane, 1989) was at least partly responsible for the fact that the degree of deregulation has been
slower in Europe than in the US, there have nevertheless been
significant regulatory changes especially in the European
Community (Gardener, 1992b). These range from the abolition
of capital and exchange controls (Padoa-Schioppa, 1987; Artis,
1988) over the 1986 'Big Bang' in the London stock market (e.g.
Mayer, 1992; Llewellyn, 1990) to the creation of a single
European financial space characterised by minimum harmonisation of key regulatory areas such as capital adequacy and deposit insurance, a regime of mutual recognition of banks' licences

among EC countries and host country supervision of internationally operating institutions (Fitchew, 1990a,b; Hawawini and Rajera, 1990; Neven, 1992, Steinherr and Gilibert, 1989).

Against this background of gradual regulatory liberalisation, banks have engaged in a process of internationalisation in the wholesale and investment banking area which has led to entry of many foreign financial institutions into domestic markets. Internationalisation received a further boost by technological advances facilitating international communication, linking capital markets and allowing computer-based trading. Foreign entry led to significantly increased competition, resulting in lower margins and profits in this sector. Especially Japanese banks entering the European market operated with extremely low margins forcing indigenous institutions to cut down prices and commissions as a response (Dueser, 1991).

International lending decreased as a result of the capital adequacy guidelines of the Bank for International Settlements (BIS), however, which took full effect at the end of 1992 (BIS, 1987; Gardener, 1992). The BIS rules have impacted the industry by reducing uncontrolled asset growth, increasing the focus on quality lending and forcing banks to raise new capital. The impact of the capital requirements was probably most significant in the US, where a number of banks had to engage in substantial restructuring including the shedding of subsidiaries to reduce total assets, and in Japan where the volatile stock market has led to difficulties of meeting the new guidelines. In Europe, however, the vast majority of banks had no difficulties in meeting the BIS requirements.

The standing of commercial banks in the corporate lending market has also been impacted by an increasing trend towards disintermediation (Gardener and Molyneux, 1990; Bryan, 1991). This phenomenon, which originated in the US, refers to the fact that large corporates bypass banks as their main source of external funds and instead tap capital markets directly without using a financial intermediary. The rise of the commercial paper market is so far the most conspicuous symptom of this trend in Europe (Acheson and Halstead, 1991).

Banking has been further affected by the rise in loan defaults and the resulting need to provide significant funds as bad debt provisions. While at the beginning of the 1980s bad debt provisions for third-world loans dominated, at the beginning of the

1990s with the economic downturn in most European countries and the accompanying rise in company failures and the fall in real estate prices, banks were increasingly forced to provide substantial bad debt provisions for their commercial as well as their retail lending. With the number of loan defaults increasing, lending activities have become increasingly risky and risk-adjusted returns have decreased accordingly. In conjunction with increasing volatility in capital and currency markets, banks' traditional operating environment has therefore become increasingly volatile and less predictable.

Despite this difficult operating environment, banks' profitability has so far not been adversely affected in most EC countries. Figure 1.1 shows the return on assets for the period from 1980 to 1990.

Figure 1.1: Return on assets for commercial banks in the EC, Japan and the US from 1980 to 1990

Return on assets

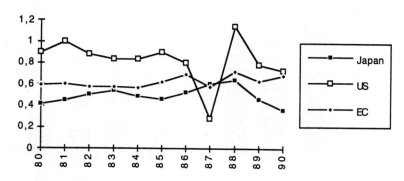

Source: data were taken from the OECD's annual bank profitability statistics (OECD, 1992b) and the return on assets is calculated as profit before tax (but after bad debt provisions) divided by total assets.

Unadjusted accounting data are notoriously difficult to compare because of the different accounting, legal and regulatory environments. Spanish banks, for example, provide fairly high bad debt provisions, reducing reported operating profits, while German banks may have large hidden reserves which do not appear in published accounts. Danish banks, on the other hand, are required to value security holdings at current market prices at the end of each financial year which leads to significant fluctuations in operating profits.

With these qualifications in mind, figure 1.1 shows that the return on assets has remained fairly stable in the EC countries, Japan and the US, with a falling trend towards the end of the 1980s in the US and Japan after a peak was reached in 1988. In the EC countries, the return on assets even increased in tendency towards the end of the 1980s. While operating results for the years 1991 and 1992 have been less favourable in some countries such as the UK and France, the EC countries in general have so far escaped the dramatic fall in operating profitability which has taken place in the Nordic countries due to high loan defaults or the high number of insolvencies which characterised the Savings and Loans crisis in the US.

Figure 1.2: Number of inhabitants per bank branch in 1989/90

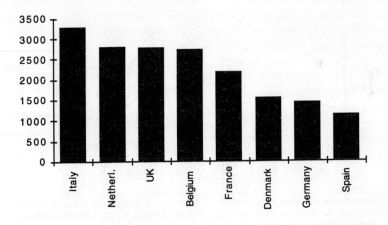

Source: OECD (1989, p. 127; 1991); Denmark: Annual Statistical Yearbook; Germany: Deutsche Bundesbank; France: de Boissieu (1990, p. 12); Italy: Lane (1991); UK (data include building societies): Bank for International Settlements, Statistics on Payment Systems.

In retail banking, which shall be defined as encompassing the markets for personal customers as well as small businesses, the branch is still the predominant route of distribution. Figure 1.2 illustrates the density of retail branch networks in the EC countries. It shows significant differences in the number of inhabitants served by a particular branch. While Germany, Denmark and Spain have a particularly low number of residents per branch, Italy has the lowest branch density although quickly catching up after branch openings were partly liberalised by the Italian Central Bank in 1990 (Lane, 1991).

Table 1.3 shows that those countries with the highest branch density also had the largest growth rate of domestic branches since the 1960s. In particular, the case of Spain stands out where the number of branches has almost tripled since 1960. It is also apparent that in most countries the level of branches has stabilised since 1980 and in some cases has even started to decline again. In the UK, for example, there has been a tangible decrease in the number of bank branches. The big four clearing banks have cut down their branch network from a peak of more than 10,200 in 1987 to around 8,800 in 1992 (Gapper, 1993c). This illustrates that banks are becoming increasingly cost-conscious and thoroughly analyse the contribution margin of each individual branch. Small and unprofitable branches may be closed or merged in areas where cluster configuration and multiple outlets allow such rationalisation.

Table 1.3: Number of Branches in 8 EC countries from 1960 to 1990

	1960	1970	1980	1990	CAGR
Spain	n.a.	12,600	24,600	34,500*	+4.9%
France	n.a.	15,000	23,700	25,600*	+2.6%
Italy	9,200	10,800	12,200	17,700	+2.4%
Belgium	1,900	3,200	3,800	3,600	+0.7%
Germany	30,000	40,800	44,700	44,000	+0.4%
Netherl.	3,500	5,200	7,400	5,400	+0.2%
Denmark	2,400	3,500	3,700	3,300	-0.2%
UK	n.a.	n.a.	19,800	20,600	n.a.

Note: all data are without Postbank outlets; * data are for 1989; CAGR = Compound Annual Growth Rate calculated from 1970 ; figures are rounded to the nearest hundred
Source: same sources as figure 1.2.

In addition to streamlining their branch networks, banks have significantly changed the design and strategic objectives of their branches. Rather than being purely service units which serve the transaction requirements of customers, branches are increasingly designated as sales centres with the stated objective of meeting specified sales and profit targets. To meet this objective, branches are becoming more open in terms of design and architecture and look increasingly like regular retail shops, replacing the traditional lay-out of customers queuing in small areas and being served by cashiers sitting behind safety glass. Back-office functions are increasingly taken out of branches and are being centralised in a few regional centres. Remaining branch staff focus on selling products, rather than administrative functions. Several banks now stratify their customers according to profit potential and serve customer sub-segments through different bank advisers.

The opportunity to stratify customers has been facilitated by advances in information technology which allow systematic analyses of the customer base according to set criteria. One of the most significant competitive advantages of banks compared to insurance companies is the depth and quality of information which banks possess. This stems from the fact that banks can analyse payment streams which may reveal a significant amount of information about the customer including net salary, outstanding debt or assets available for investment. Information technology not only permits such systematic scanning of the customer base for selling leads but has also led to improvements in the speed and quality of service which bank staff can provide to customers. It has significantly altered the skills profile of bank employees, since many tasks and information requirements which formerly needed to be provided manually by bank staff are now automated and can be supplied by PC-supported information systems.

Both the new design of retail branches as well as the introduction of greater IT-support in the branches require significant investment outlays, and therefore banks increasingly strive to make optimal use of their high-fixed cost retail network. They are therefore scanning the spectrum of financial products to select those which combine high customer benefits with profit potential for the bank. During this process of product scanning, a number of banks have identified insurance and most especially life products as offering high profit potential with low associated risk.

In summary, this section showed that European banking is characterised by an increasingly competitive and risky operating environment. Against this background, banks form the decision to enter the area of insurance. The next section presents aggregate data on entry activities of European banks into insurance.

3. Entry of European banks into insurance: aggregate data

An analysis of entry activities of the largest 60 EC banks reveals that the majority is now involved in bancassurance. A scrutiny of annual reports for 1991 reveals that 35 of the largest 60 EC banks were involved in bancassurance, while 25 banks had no insurance interests. Of these 35 banks more than 80 per cent had entered life insurance only, 5 per cent had entered non-life insurance only, while 13 per cent had entered both life and non-life business.

Banks have entered the insurance market through 14 joint ventures, 12 de novo entries, 10 acquisitions or mergers and 4 distribution alliances.[5] The database is shown in table 1.4.

Table 1.4: Entry activities of the largest 60 EC banks

Joint ventures

Bank	Insurer	Year
Deutsche Bank, Germany, $11.3 billion	Gerling, Germany	1989
National Westminster, UK, $10.5 billion	Clerical and Medical, UK	1993
Banco Central Hispanoamericano, Spain, $6.5 billion	Aetna Life, US	n.a.
Istituto Bancario San Paolo di Torino, Italy, $6 billion	Fondiaria, Italy	1991
Cariplo, Italy, $6.0 billion and TSB, UK, $3.1 billion	Caisse National de Prevoyance, France	1990
Commerzbank, Germany $5.5 billion	Deutsche Beamtenversicherung, Germany	1990
Banesto, Spain, $4,5 billion	Groupe AG, Belgium	n.a.
Midland Bank, UK, $4.3 billion	Commercial Union, UK	1987
Banca Commerciale Italiana, Italy, $3.9 billion	Generali, Italy	n.a.
Banco Santander, Spain, $3.8 billion	Metropolitan Life, US	1987
Credito Italiano, Italy, $3.1 billion	Commercial Union, UK	1990
Royal Bank of Scotland, UK, $2.8 billion	Scottish Equitable, UK	1990
Banque Indosuez, France, $2.3 billion	Mapfre, Spain	1989

| Banco Popular Espanol, Spain, $2.1 billion | Allianz, Germany | 1989 |

Distribution alliances

Bank	Insurer	Year
Banque National de Paris, France, $10.2 billion	UAP, France	1989
Dresdner Bank, Germany, $6.5 billion	Allianz, Germany	1989
DG Bank. Germany $2.4 billion	Allianz, Germany	1989
Bank of Scotland, UK, $2.1 billion	Standard Life, UK	1989

De novo entry

Bank	Subsidiary	Year
Credit Agricole, France, $14.7 billion	Predica	1986
Barclays Bank, UK, 11.7 billion	Barclays Life	1969
Deutsche Bank, Germany, $11.3 billion	Deutsche Leben	1989
Compagnie Financiere de Paribas, France, $10.5 billion	Cardif	1973
Credit Lyonnais, France, $10.5 billion	UAF	1985
BNP, France, $10.2 billion	Natio Vie	1985
Societe Generale, France, $7.1 billion	Sogecap	1972
Banco Bilbao Vizcaya, Spain, $6.2 billion	Euroseguros	1982
Banca Nazionale del Lavoro, Italy, $5.5 billion	Lavoro Vita	1986
Credit Mutuel Confederation National, France, $4.2 billion	ACM Vie	1970
Den Danske Bank, Denmark, $3.5 billion	subsidiary	n.a.
TSB Group, UK, $3.1 billion	TSB Life	1967

Mergers and majority acquisitions

Bank	Insurer	Year
Deutsche Bank, Germany, $11.3 billion	Deutscher Herold	1992
NMB Postbank, Netherl., $8.1 billion	Nationale Nederlanden	1991
Rabobank, Netherl. $7.6 billion	Interpolis	1990
Cariplo, Italy, $6.0 billion	Fata	n.a.
Lloyds Bank, UK, $4.8 billion	Abbey Life	1988
Hypo-Bank, Germany, $3.9 billion	Allianz	1988
TSB Group, UK, $3.1 billion	Target Life, Hill Hammond	1987
Unibank, Denmark, $2.6 billion	Tryg Forsikring	1991
CIC-Union Europeenne, France, 2.6 billion	GAN	1990
BfG Bank, Germany, $1.9 billion	A&M Group	1987

Banks are ordered according to their size of capital taken from the July 1992 edition of *The Banker*.

Source: own compilation from annual reports; press clippings; The Banker.

This database constitutes the basic framework for selecting the case studies in part two of the study. Since the analysis has shown that 95 per cent of banks which have entered insurance have chosen life insurance, the next section provides an industry-level analysis of incentives to enter this sector.

4. Incentives for banks to enter life insurance: industry-level factors

When assessing the option to enter life insurance, banks need to take into account a variety of economic, demographic and strategic factors. This section analyses the incentives for banks to enter the life insurance market from an industry perspective, while the next section discusses firm-level reasons for entering insurance.

This section focuses on the six key factors which influence banks' decision whether to enter the life insurance sector:
- demographic changes
- economic environment
- savings trends
- differential tax treatment
- growth performance and potential
- insurance penetration and saturation.

These factors are summarised in figure 1.3. The next sections discuss each of these forces in turn.

4.1. Demographic factors

First, consider the demographic changes which have taken place in the Western industrialised countries over the past decades. Figure 1.4 presents population growth rates, i.e. the percentage change in the total number of residents from 1950 to 1990 in the EC countries as well as in Japan and the US. From the figure it becomes apparent that population growth rates have slowed significantly since the 1950s and 1960s. While population size in the EC grew by 8.5 per cent between 1950 and 1960, this rate had slowed down to 2.6 per cent in the 1980s. Similar, though less dramatic trends could be observed in Japan and the US where population growth rates have halved since the 1950s.

Figure 1.3: Industry-level incentives for banks to enter life insurance

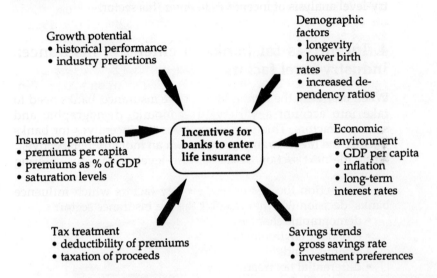

The reason for the dramatic decline in population growth rates is the decrease in birth rates which has taken place in all industrialised Western countries. With the introduction of birth control measures and changes in lifestyle, the average number of children per household has declined considerably. As a result, the birth rate is not sufficiently high to sustain even a stable population size. The fact that population numbers have not actually started falling as yet is solely due to the fact that non-EC workers have moved into EC countries, while immigration has also increased significantly. This trend is likely to continue as immigrants enter the EC and Eastern Europe may provide a large pool of workers willing to move to the EC countries.

Lower birth rates will have a significant impact on the age structure of the population over the next decades. The proportion of younger people becomes smaller, while the number of elderly increases. As a result, the 'dependency ratio', i.e. the number of retirees which must be supported by the working population is set to rise dramatically.

Figure 1.5 reports the age structure of the EC countries between 1960 and 1990 and provides a prediction until the year 2020. It becomes apparent that the proportion of those above the age of 60 increases dramatically from 15 per cent in 1960 to 27 per cent in 2020. The proportion of those aged above 80 has already increased from 1.6 per cent in 1960 to 3.4 per cent in 1990. At the same time, the number of those below 19 years of age will fall from over 30 per cent in 1960 to around 20 per cent in the year 2020.

Figure 1.4: Population growth rates in the EC countries, Japan and the US from 1950 to 1990

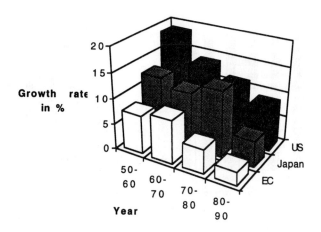

Source: Eurostat (1992).

As a result, according to projections by the OECD, the dependency ratio is likely to increase from a current level of around 21 per cent for the EC as a whole to 37 per cent in the year 2030. This means that the number of people aged 65 or older will constitute close to 40 per cent of the working population by the middle of the next century. As a result, there is likely to be an increasing strain on public pension systems and a per-

ceived need to engage in additional retirement provisions to secure living standards.

Life insurance companies can successfully exploit this trend by
focusing on demographic changes in their marketing activities.
Longevity and the desire to maintain accustomed living standards after retirement can be employed as strong selling arguments for life insurance products.

**Figure 1.5: Age structure of population in the EC between 1960
and 2020**

Percentage
of Population in Age Group

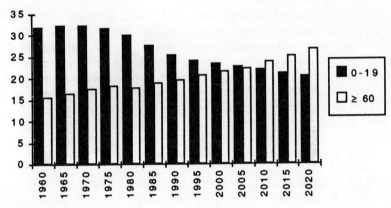

Source: Eurostat (1992).

In addition to lower birth rates, life expectancy has also increased dramatically in the EC countries due to advances in
medical research and care. Life expectancy at birth in 1989 for
the EC as a whole was 73 years for men and 79 years for women.
In Japan it is 75 years for men and 81 years for women, while in
the US it is 72 years for men and 79 years for women (Eurostat,
1992). Life expectancy in the EC since 1960, for example, has
therefore increased by six years for both men and women.

The increase in life expectancy was unevenly distributed
across the EC countries. Since 1960 average life expectancy for

men has increased between 2 years in Denmark and 10 years for Portugal. For women life expectancy has increased by 3 and 11 years respectively in these two countries.

The fact that women, on average, have a greater life expectancy than men leads to increased need for financial security for households where the man is the only wage-earner. This fact is frequently used by life insurers as a selling argument for term life insurance with marketing campaigns which usually centre around the theme of "ensuring financial security for your family".

In summary, demographic changes taking place in the Western industrialised countries are likely to lead to a dramatic increase in the proportion of the elderly relative to the working population which is likely to place a strain on public pension systems which finance themselves through contributions of the working population.

An important buying criterion for life insurance is therefore the type and reliability of national public pension provisions. Demand for life insurance is influenced by the trust which the public places in public schemes as well as specific provisions and regulations. While all EC countries have some form of public pension scheme which form the centre of social security systems, specific regulations differ between individual countries.

Public pension systems finance themselves through contributions by employees which are usually dependent on income. They provide payments which can reach up to 75 per cent of the salary earned just before retirement such as in France if contributions have been made for the maximum number of years possible. In particular, for higher-income groups, however, public schemes frequently do not provide the desired level of income after retirement, since in most countries there are maximum payout rates which may fall well short of the income earned before retirement. In addition, public schemes usually only provide sufficient financial stability if the employee has made payments for a considerable number of years. As a result, in case of early retirement or early death, the level of provisions for the retiree and his family is frequently not sufficient to secure the standard of living.

Complementing public pension schemes, company pension schemes frequently provide additional pension payments for employees which vary between 15 and 25 per cent of the payments of the public pension scheme.

A thorough analysis of the type of public and company-level retirement schemes is therefore required for banks assessing the economic potential of life insurance. In particular, a careful analysis of pay-out ratios after retirement, the possibility to contract out of the public scheme and an analysis of customer groups which may not be adequately covered by a public scheme to secure their accomplished standard of living needs to be undertaken to assess the prospects of life insurance.

4.2. Economic environment

When assessing the business potential of entering life insurance, a bank needs to take into account a number of economic variables. Acquiring a whole life insurance policy, for example, is a long-term investment decision which is significantly influenced by the economic environment in which consumers and life insurers operate. In general, the demand for life insurance is influenced by a number of economic variables including GDP per capita, inflation, long-term real interest rates and savings ratios.

First, consider gross domestic product (GDP) per capita which gives an indication of the relative economic wealth of the country's residents. In general, there is some degree of correlation between GDP levels and life insurance premiums, as the demand for life insurance increases, in tendency, with the relative economic wealth of the country's inhabitants. Lechner and Enz (1993), for example, report a simple regression of the form $y = a + bx$ where y are real life insurance premium growth rates and x stands for real GDP growth rates. Regressing data for 52 countries over the time period 1981 to 91, they find a beta-value of 1.35 (R-square: 0.9) which implies that life insurance premiums increase over-proportionately, as GDP rises.

Figure 1.6 shows GDP per capita in ECU for the EC countries, Japan and the US for 1989. These figures were adjusted in order to account for purchasing power disparities and even out exchange rate fluctuations. It becomes obvious that there are quite distinct differences between individual EC countries with Luxembourg and Germany leading the EC ranking with GDP rates of ECU 22,300 and ECU 19,200 (purchasing-power-adjusted) respectively in 1989. Portugal and Greece had less than half these ratios with ECU 9,500 and ECU 9,400 respectively. The highest GDP per capita ratio was achieved in the US, however, with ECU 26,500 in 1989. Japan had a slightly higher GDP per resident level than Germany.

Figure 1.6: GDP per capita in EC countries, Japan and the US in 1989

Purchasing power index

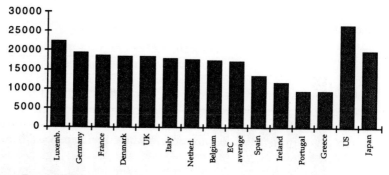

Source: Eurostat (1992).

GDP growth rates have slowed down in the EC countries in the 1980s with most countries in recession in 1993. While the average GDP growth rate at constant market prices stood at 3 per cent in the second half of the 1970s, it slowed to less than 2 per cent in the 1980s. For 1993 growth rates are likely to be negative for the majority of EC countries. As a result of the correlation between GDP growth rates and life insurance premiums, growth rates of premiums are therefore likely to slow down as well.

Another significant factor influencing the economic potential of life insurance is the level of inflation. Low inflation rates and expectations are a necessary prerequisite for stable returns on long-term investment such as life insurance. When expectations concerning the real level of inflation are high, consumers are unlikely to invest in long-term products due to fears of negative returns.

Figure 1.7 shows inflation rates for the EC countries, Japan and the US between 1985 and 1992. During this period, consumer prices in the EC rose by 49 per cent, more than the price increases in the US with 30 per cent and Japan with only 12 per cent. Price increases also varied significantly between the EC countries ranging from 11 per cent in the Netherlands to 208 per cent in Greece.

Figure 1.7: Inflation rates for EC countries, Japan and the US between 1985 and 1992

Index: 1985=100

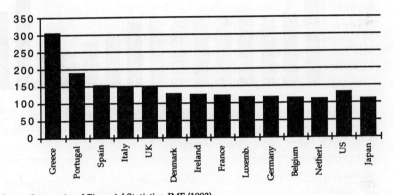

Source: International Financial Statistics, IMF (1993).

In the first quarter of 1993 this order was only slightly changed with the increases in the consumer price index having gone up in Germany to 4.3 per cent, while inflation rates in the UK and France had fallen to 1.9 per cent and 2.2 per cent respectively.

While there are still significant differences between inflation rates of individual EC countries, the discipline imposed by the European exchange rate mechanism (ERM) on its member countries has led to some degree of convergence. In the second half of the 1970s, for example, inflation rates stood at 4 per cent in Germany, compared to more than 16 per cent in Italy, 14 per cent in the UK and 10 per cent in France. Effectively, the restrictive monetary policy of the German Bundesbank, the *de facto* anchor of the ERM, forced the other ERM members to engage in anti-inflationary policies. Considering the present difficulties which the ERM faces, it remains to be seen whether this anti-inflationary course will continue in the future.

4.3. Changing savings trends

The gross savings rate of private households expresses total savings of households as a percentage of GDP and constitutes the total potential for life insurance. Amongst this pool of savings, life insurance competes with other long-term savings products such as government bonds or investment funds.

Figure 1.8 shows gross savings rates in 6 EC countries from 1970 to 1990. It becomes obvious that gross savings rates differ significantly across the EC countries. Italy has by far the highest savings rate with more than 16 per cent of GDP in 1990, while the UK, Spain and the Netherlands have lower rates than the EC average which stood at slightly more than 9 per cent in 1990. The UK, in fact, had the lowest savings ratio with only 3.5 per cent.

Savings trends have changed significantly over time in the EC countries. Most notable is the increasing significance of life insurance as a form of saving for private households. In particular, life insurance accounts for an increasing share of total savings in some EC countries which underlines its rising significance and the successful inroads which insurers were able to make into the savings pool which, traditionally, was virtually monopolised by banks.

Unfortunately, no consistent data on the share of life insurance in total savings are available for the EC which would allow a comparison over time and across countries. I therefore analyse the examples of Germany and France for which satisfactory data were available.

German banks have witnessed a significant reduction in their traditional funding base, particularly savings and demand deposits which decreased from 65 per cent in 1960 of total household savings to less than 40 per cent in 1990. This dramatic decline is partly explained by the low interest rates which are paid on savings accounts in Germany inducing many savers to switch into higher-yielding short-term deposits. Over the same time period, life insurance has increased its share of total savings by almost 40 per cent to more than 20 per cent in 1990.

Figure 1.8: Gross savings rates of private households for 6 EC countries from 1970 to 1990

Total savings as
per cent of GDP

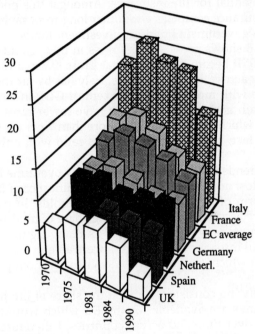

Source: Eurostat (1992).

In France an even more drastic erosion of savings deposits could be observed in the 1980s. As is shown in figure 1.9, insurance has dramatically increased its share of total savings from less than 10 per cent in 1980 to more than 45 per cent in 1990. In fact, investment in life insurance now constitutes the highest share of total savings of private households in France.

Figure 1.9: Analysis of monetary assets of private households in France from 1980 to 1990

Share of
total savings in %

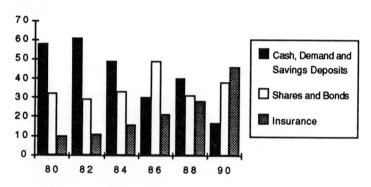

Source: Swiss Reinsurance/Sigma 2/92.

Similar developments can be observed in other European countries where life insurance has increasingly become a form of saving and is thereby cutting into the share of monetary assets which were traditionally deposited with banks. Thus, banks are witnessing a steady erosion of their deposit base. Since retail deposits constitute the cheapest source of funds for banks, it is therefore natural for banks to start considering whether they, too, could enter the sector of life insurance or even reverse the trend of losing market share in total savings to life insurers. A further important criterion why life insurance products are frequently preferred to traditional bank savings products is the preferential tax treatment which they are granted. This is the issue to which I turn in the next section.

4.4. Tax treatment of life insurance

The choice between traditional savings instruments of banks and life insurance policies may be significantly influenced by tax considerations. Life insurance is frequently supported by an advantageous tax regime. This stems from the public policy objective to encourage personal protection and retirement planning in order to reduce the burden on public pension retirement systems. Tax treatment of life insurance varies significantly across the EC countries, however. A comprehensive analysis of the intricacies of tax regulations governing life insurance in individual countries would certainly exceed the scope of this study. Table 1.5 therefore provides only a brief overview of the differing regulations in the EC countries.

Table 1.5: Tax treatment of life insurance in the EC

	Tax Relief on Premiums p.a. (1)	Tax on Proceeds
Belgium	15% of first ECU1,250, 6% of next ECU15,500, 25% of next ECU1,125	no tax after 10 years
Denmark	None	no tax on endowment assurance
France	25% of savings element up to ECU670 of endowment policies	endowment assurance tax-free after 6 years, capitalisation after 8 years
Germany	Up to ECU3,600	no tax after 12 years of policy duration
Greece	50% up to ECU 2,400	not available
Ireland	50% up to ECU2,500	not available
Italy	Up to ECU1,400	12.5% on profits
Luxemb.	Up to ECU 680	not available
Netherl.	Only for annuity policies	tax-free after 12 years
Portugal	Against complementary tax only	tax-free
Spain	10% of up to 30% of taxable income	20% of proceeds, source tax
UK	Only on qualifying pension plans	tax-free

Notes: (1) Limits for premium relief are given on the basis of a jointly assessed married couple.
Source: own compilation from Salomon Brothers (1990), Price Waterhouse, Swiss Reinsurance/Sigma 2/92.

One of the most significant decision variables for the personal customer when acquiring a whole life policy as opposed to purchasing term life insurance and investing in a long-term investment fund is whether life premiums can be deducted from income taxes. Some form of tax deductibility for life premiums is provided in most EC countries with the exception of Denmark, the UK and the Netherlands. Such tax advantages may constitute the single most important criterion for buying whole life insurance.

The second major tax advantage granted to life insurance is that unlike for interest payments of government bonds or in-

vestment funds, proceeds for life insurance policies are tax-free
in most EC countries after a minimum duration of the life policy.
Thus, they are not subject to a withholding tax which is applicable to proceeds from other savings and investment products
and can range up to 25 per cent in the UK and 30 per cent in
Germany, for example.

One of the critical factors which determines future demand
for life insurance is therefore the prevailing tax regime and the
question whether it will continue to enjoy the current tax benefits. While deregulation has taken place in the UK and the
Netherlands, for example, where some tax advantages of life insurance were recently abolished, it seems likely that continued
strain on public pension systems will induce policymakers to further encourage private retirement provision and continue to
provide tax incentives for such products in most countries.

4.5. Insurance penetration and saturation

The relative importance of the life insurance industry varies significantly across countries. As illustrated in figure 1.10, the
United Kingdom and Ireland have the highest share of life insurance expressed as a percentage of GDP with 7 per cent and
5.4 per cent respectively in 1991. The Southern European countries, in contrast, have the lowest share of life premiums in total
GDP with Greece, Italy, Spain and Portugal ranking at the bot-
tom with less than one per cent.

A related though different measure of the relative significance of the insurance sector in an economy is to look at the ab-
solute amount which residents spend on insurance premiums per
annum. Annual premiums per capita in $US are shown in figure
1.11. The UK leads the ranking where a resident, on average,
spends $1,320 on life insurance premiums in 1991. The
Netherlands come second with $940, followed by France with
$770 and Ireland with $730. The average Greek, in contrast,
spends only $57 on life insurance.

4.6. Growth performance of the insurance industry

A significant criterion for banks deciding whether or not to enter insurance is the growth performance and potential of the industry. While banking has become a fairly saturated market in

most EC countries with low or even negative growth rates, premium increases in life insurance have been significant in most EC countries. Figure 1.11 shows growth rates for the EC economies, Japan and the US for both non-life and life insurance.

Figure 1.10: Insurance penetration in EC economies, Japan and US in 1991

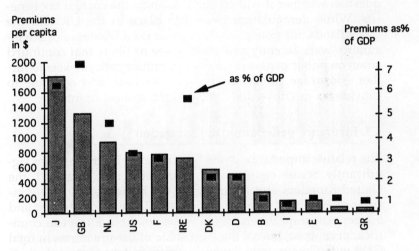

Source: Swiss Reinsurance/Sigma 4/1993.

A comparison of growth rates of life and non-life premiums shows that growth in life insurance has been significantly greater than in non-life business in all surveyed countries except Belgium and Ireland. Growth in life insurance has been especially strong in the Mediterranean countries such as Spain, Portugal, France, Italy and Greece which have for a long time been under-developed in the life insurance field. But even in markets which are relatively saturated such as the UK or Germany, growth rates of life premiums have been significant outpacing those of general insurance.

Figure 1.11: Average premium growth rates in life and non-life insurance for EC economies, Japan and US from 1986 to 1991

Annual growth
rate in %

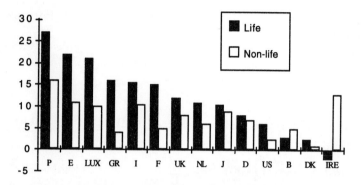

Source: own calculation from Swiss Reinsurance/Sigma, several issues.

In terms of total size, the largest EC life insurance market in terms of total premiums is the UK with 1991 premiums of almost $75 billion and France with $44 billion, followed by Germany with $40 billion and the Netherlands with $14. The European market was dwarfed by the size of the US and Japanese markets, however, which alone account for almost 60 per cent of life insurance premiums worldwide. The US has premiums of $202 billion, while Japan accounts for $226 billion in 1991.

Projections by industry experts continue to predict an upward growth trend for life premiums, as demand is likely to increase further. As explained in this section, increasing strains on public pension systems, rising wealth and corresponding changes in consumer behaviour, tax advantages granted to life insurance and demographic changes leading to a dramatic rise of the proportion of retired as part of the total population are likely to provide a continuous stimulus for the demand of life insurance.

While the analysis has made clear that one needs to differentiate carefully between individual countries, since institutional arrangements vary significantly, it appears that overall the growth prospects for the life insurance industry continue to be excellent. A study by Arthur Andersen (Andersen, 1990), for example, predicts growth rates of 5 to 9 per cent in the 1990s in life insurance for Europe as a whole, while envisioning growth in Southern Europe in excess of 10 per cent and even greater than 15 per cent for specific products in countries such as Portugal and Spain.

Having analysed industry-level incentives for banks to enter the insurance sector in this section, the next section provides a firm-level analysis of economic incentives.

5. Incentives for banks to enter insurance: firm-level factors

The most important firm-level factor on the part of banks for entering insurance business is the existence of synergy effects between banking and insurance. This section analyses such synergy effects and assess in which areas of the business system these effects are likely to play the most significant role.

Synergy effects are usually summarised by the simple statement that "2 plus 2 equals 5". In other words, combing two separate business units or two companies leads to a level of profits for the combined entity which exceeds the sum of profits of the two separate organizations. The next section provides a more precise definition of synergy effects, while sections 5.2 and 5.3 look at the potential of scale and scope economies.

5.1. Synergy effects: a definition

There are several definitions of synergy in the management literature. The definition which has received the widest popularity is that of Ansoff (1965). Let the annual return on investment (ROI) for product i with $i = 1, ..., n$ be defined as

(1) $ROI_i = R_i - C_i / I_i$

where R_i is the annual revenue of the i'th product, C_i are annual costs and I_i is the investment outlay. If there are no synergy effects between individual products then the following equation holds for the return on investment, ROI_F, of the multi-product firm:

(2) $ROI_F = \sum ROI_i$

If synergy effects are present, then there is at least one interdependency between the three variables in equation (1). Thus, if we compare an integrated multi-product firm with a firm which consists only of completely independent units then synergy effects occur if either of the following three conditions hold for the integrated firm:
- for a given level of revenue, investment and/or costs are lower;
- for a given level of investment, revenues are greater and/or costs are lower;
- for a given level of costs, investment is lower and/or revenues are greater.

In other words, if synergy effects are present then the ROI for an integrated firm is higher than for a firm which consists only of independent business units.[6] As this definition illustrates, synergy can be divided into cost-, revenue- and investment-effects. The next two sections discuss the two most frequent causes which may lead to synergy. These are economies of scale referring to decreasing costs as the scale of output increases and economies of scope which occur when costs are lower for a multi-product firm compared to stand-alone units.

5.2. Economies of scale

Economies of scale are frequently cited as the economic rationale for mergers between financial institutions. They may also convey a competitive advantage to those firms which operate at lower cost levels purely due to greater size. In the context of bancassurance, economies of scale are frequently referred to as providing advantages to large institutions, in particular in areas such as asset management and back-office functions. Scale advantages in this area may arise from spreading overheads over a larger income or result from greater market power which reduces operating costs due to lock-in effects of customers and lower commissions which need to be paid to fund managers. In addition to purely economic explanations, size considerations often play an important role in managerial objective functions, as larger size is usually associated with greater power and status. National rankings of financial institutions according to size and the strategic objective "to become (one of) the largest banks or insurers" contribute to a significant role attributed to pure balance sheet size.

Formally, for single-output production, scale economies refer to decreasing long-run average costs, as the scale of activity increases. In the case of a multiproduct firm, scale effects are defined either as ray economies or product-specific economies.

Ray economies of scale measure cost behaviour of a proportionate output change as the composition of the output bundle remains unchanged.[7] For a multiproduct output vector Q, ray average costs are defined as $C(aQ)/a$, where a is a scalar of the level of output. Ray economies of scale are then defined as

$$(3) \qquad S_r = C(Q)/\Sigma Q_i MC_i$$

where S_r greater, equal or smaller than one implies increasing, constant or decreasing returns to scale.

To measure product-specific scale economies, Bailey and Friedlaender (1982) introduce average incremental costs (AIC). For the two-product case these are defined for each product as follows:

$$(4) \qquad AIC_1 = C(Q_1, Q_2) - C(0, Q_2)/Q_1$$

i.e. average incremental costs for the first product are total costs less the costs of not producing commodity 1, divided by its output (analogously for the second good). Product-specific returns to scale are then given by:

$$(5) \qquad S_i = AIC_1(Q)/MC_i$$

Again, S_i greater, equal or smaller one implies increasing, constant or decreasing returns to scale.

Two main sources of scale economies in financial services can be distinguished: production and financial scale economies.

Production scale economies refer to spreading fixed costs over a larger scale of activities. Fixed costs may occur, for example, by maintaining a retail branch network whose costs may be fixed in the short run.

Financial scale economies, on the other hand, may result from diversification advantages: generally, as the scale of activity increases, the financial firm can diversify across risky assets and liabilities, and thereby reduce the variance of earnings at a constant level of expected returns. For example, as the number of depositors increases, the variability of withdrawals is reduced and proportionately fewer liquid reserves need to be held.

Existing empirical evidence does not confirm the significance of economies of scale in banking, however, with more recent studies even providing evidence for diseconomies beyond a certain activity level (e.g. Athanasios, Subhash and Miller, 1990). Typically, the estimated cost function displays a U-shaped form with most major size economies exhausted at a capital size of around ECU 50 million (e.g. Berger *et al.*, 1987; Mester, 1987; Dermine and Röller, 1991; Rodriguez *et al.*, 1993).

Possibly most interestingly, all studies find significant differences in terms of average costs between firms of the same size. For the insurance sector, Imfeld (1991) shows that average costs as a percentage of premiums range from 5 percent to 65 percent for firms of the *same* size in several countries examined. Prosperetti (1991) shows that in the Italian insurance sector this figure ranges from 15 to 110 percent. Similarly in the banking sector, Berger and Humphrey (1991) stratify a sample of US banks according to size and find that cost differences among banks in the same size cluster are significant and may average up to 34 percent.

These results suggest that efficiency issues may be much more important than scale economies. Thus, a firm which is large may at the same time be inefficient and therefore have lower profits than a highly efficient small firm. It seems that profitability in financial services has much less to do with pure size than with internal efficiency. In the context of bancassurance this implies that entry moves of banks into insurance cannot be justified by size considerations. While there may be some economies of scale in the area of asset management, such effects are exhausted at a fairly low scale and are certainly not significant enough to single-handedly justify entry into insurance. Mergers between banks and insurers are therefore unlikely to provide economic benefits solely due to increased firm size. The next section analyses scope economies which are probably the most important cause of synergy effects in the area of bancassurance.

5.3. Economies of scope

Bancassurance involves multiproduct services and is most frequently justified with the existence of economies of scope between banking and insurance.[8] Formally, these are defined as follows: let Q_b be an output vector of $i = 1,...,n$ products. A cost function is then called strictly sub-additive if

$$(6) \quad C \left(\Sigma Q_i \right) < \Sigma C \left(Q_i \right)$$

for all Q such that $\Sigma Q_i > 0$. For the two product case, economies of scope exist for a strictly sub-additive cost function if

$$(7) \quad C \left(Q_1, Q_2 \right) < C \left(0, Q_1 \right) + C \left(Q_2, 0 \right)$$

where $C \left(0, Q_1 \right)$ and $C \left(Q_2, 0 \right)$ are called stand-alone costs. This implies that the cost of jointly offering services Q_1 and Q_2 is smaller than offering them separately.

Berger *et al.* (1987) note that scope effects arising from increased revenue due to product expansion may not immediately feed through to the cost function. Similarly, increased lock-in effects which result from expanding into insurance may be difficult to detect when estimating the cost function. Statistical estimates of the cost function are therefore likely to underestimate the long-term effect of scope economies, as the impact on revenues is only insufficiently captured. Thus, it may be the case that the cost function actually displays *dis*economies of scope, while profits rise as the number of products increases because the revenue-enhancing effect outweighs the cost increase. In order to take account of this problem, I introduce the concept of *revenue* scope effects. For the two-product case and a given cost level, revenue scope effects exist if:

$$(8) \quad R \left(Q_1, Q_2 \right) > R \left(0, Q_1 \right) + R \left(Q_2, 0 \right)$$

where R(.) is the revenue function. Scope economies and revenue scope effects in the context of bancassurance may derive from five main sources:

• *Shared inputs:* common inputs may be utilised more efficiently when applied to various products, thus avoiding excess capacity.[9] Examples in bancassurance include the retail branch and agency network or information systems which may be utilised in the distribution of various financial products. Since information systems need to be tailored towards specific applications and the kind of data which need to be processed in banking are transaction-oriented while insurance data are history-oriented, synergy effects are more likely to lie in the area of hardware rather than software. Much more significant as a source of potential scope effects is the retail distribution network which can be utilised when including additional products in the product line. This stems from the fact that adding financial products to an existing distribution channel may cause only low marginal costs, since the basic infrastructure is already in place.

• *Intangible assets:* a special case of shared inputs are intangible assets such as managerial know-how, brand loyalty or reputation. Itami (1992, p. 45) defines an intangible asset with the characteristic that it "can be used in more than one area simultaneously without reducing its value in other areas." An important example is what Ansoff (1965) referred to as 'management synergy'. This refers to the fact that management may be able to draw on an experience base and accumulated know-how and can apply this expertise to the new business unit. Thus, a bank which has accumulated know-how in asset management, for example, will use this expertise when managing its life insurance funds. Similarly, bank loyalty and the established reputation of a bank may be another particularly important instance. In bancassurance, scope effects may result from banks being able to draw on their established reputation when selling insurance products to their existing clientele as well as to new customers.

• *Marketing economies:* one of the main economic rationales for bancassurance is that customers may prefer to acquire a range of financial products from a single institution, rather than maintaining relationships with a number of suppliers. For those customers who prefer such 'one-stop shopping' there are savings in transaction costs both for the customer as well as for the financial services supplier. A bank can therefore not only utilise its branch network to sell insurance but it can draw on established customer relationships and save on marketing costs which would be higher for a firm entering a new business completely from scratch.[10] There may be customers, however, who may be reluctant to 'put all their eggs into one basket' and prefer to spread their financial investments across a number of financial institutions. Thus, the significance of marketing economies is crucially dependent on customer preferences.

• *Diversification:* by expanding the product range, banks may be able to reduce risks at constant returns. This applies in particular to the case of entering life insurance which compared to loan activities, for example, offers significantly lower risk. Diversification results when risks are less than perfectly correlated. While there is some degree of interdependence between life insurance and loan activities, for example, since both are affected by the general business cycle, the correlation factor is likely to be low. For example, while banks have suffered significant loan losses in the current recession necessitating high loan write-offs, investment income by life insurers has been positively affected by booming stock markets. In the area of asset-liability management, there may be complementarities in the balance sheet structure of banks and insurers. Insurers' assets and liabilities are mostly long-term, while banks predominantly carry medium-term assets financed by short-term liabilities on their balance sheet (e.g. Diamond, 1984). Pooling activities may therefore result in a risk reduction effect. However, as discussed above, regulatory constraints in almost all countries reduce the potential benefits of asset pooling, since assets need to be clearly separated and 'ear-marked' as being either insurance or banking related.

• *Lock-in effects and switching costs:* financial services are frequently characterised by significant switching costs for customers which may lead to 'lock-in' effects with their current suppliers (e.g. Farrell, 1986; Weizsäcker, 1984).[11] By expanding the product portfolio to include insurance products, banks may be able to increase such lock-in effects and thereby reduce distribution costs resulting in scope economies. Klemperer (1987a,

1989, 1990) offers an interesting analysis of multi-product competition in the presence of 'switching costs' and brand (or firm) loyalty. In the absence of switching costs, it is well-established that firms usually act according to the 'principle of differentiation', i.e. rather than competing head-to-head (e.g. as integrated financial services 'supermarkets'), firms prefer to differentiate products, since this allows them to charge higher prices and avoid Bertrand competition (e.g. Shaked and Sutton, 1982; Neven, 1985). When consumers face switching costs, however, this result may be reversed, since lock-in effects may induce banks to offer an integrated product range in order to increase loyalty of the customer with the bank.[12] Thus, by expanding the product line to include insurance products, banks may be able to increase revenues more than increasing costs resulting in revenue scope effects.

The empirical evidence on scope economies in banking is limited to US studies and has as yet not produced clear conlusions: Murray and White (1983), Gilligan and Smirlock (1984), and Kim (1986) all find evidence for the existence of significant cost complementarities. Berger *et al.* (1987), however, scrutinise a sample of US banks with less than $1 billion in deposits and do not find evidence for scope economies. A similar insignificant result is found by Hunter *et al.* (1990) who apply the same methodology to a sample of the largest 400 US banks and Mester (1987) who analyses a sample of Savings&Loan Associations.

Negative results do not necessarily imply that scope economies are insignificant, however. As noted above, the current statistical measurement of scope economies does not take adequate account of revenue scope effects of expanding the product line and therefore cannot provide affirmative evidence of the significance of scope effects in financial services.

5.4. A comparison of synergy effects in life and general insurance

Why have banks so far predominantly chosen the life insurance sector when entering insurance? The most significant reason appears to be that the importance of synergy effects differs between life and general insurance. In general, the synergy potential between banking and insurance is likely to be greater in life than in general insurance, since distribution costs constitute a far greater proportion of total costs in life insurance than in non-life business with some analysts estimating that distribution costs in life insurance are up to five times greater than in non-life business (e.g. Potvliege *et al.*, 1992). As a result, resulting cost savings distributing insurance products through the branch network are significantly lower for general than for life insurance. In addition, assets under management are much lower in general insurance than in life business. Thus, synergy effects in the area of asset management are less significant in general than in life business.

In general insurance there is also the risk that the established relationship between banker and customer may be jeopardised, if claims handling leads to disagreement between customer and the issuer of the policy. Whereas life insurance has a fairly predictable pattern of customer-agent interaction which is similar to that of other investment-related products, general insurance involves a different type of interaction with potential disagreement about the actual pay-out or the type of risk covered. It is not uncommon to find customers disappointed about the lower than expected pay-outs when a claim is filed or to find out that the specific incidence is not covered by the insurance policy.

General insurance also has a more volatile and less predictable risk structure than life business. Bankers are less familiar with assessing general insurance risk, since unlike for life business the degree of relatedness between traditional banking activities and general insurance is low. Thus, the required investment in acquiring the know-how and the technical and actuarial skills necessary to operate successfully in non-life insurance is likely to be significant and investment synergies are likely to be minimal. This stems from the fact that key factors of success in general insurance are quite different from those in banking and life insurance. Whereas in general insurance underwriting skills, careful customer screening, risk assessment skills and cost effectiveness in claims handling are crucial, in life insurance asset management and distribution skills are the two critical factors of success.

In summary, therefore, potential synergy effects between life insurance and retail banking are significantly greater than those between general insurance and retail banking and this fact explains the predominant preference of banks to enter life rather than general insurance.

5.5. Limits to synergy effects and a possible organizational response

The fact that combining two product or business units may lead not only to positive synergy effects but can also result in cost increases and revenue decreases was recognised as early as 1937 in Coase's seminal paper on the nature of the firm where he notes that "as a firm gets larger, there may be decreasing returns to the entrepreneur function, that is, the costs of organising additional transactions within the firm may rise". It is also referred to as the 'Penrose-effect', as Penrose (1959) focused on diminishing returns of adding additional management to a firm. Economies of size, for example, encounter clear limits: as the number of services offered increases, economies of specialisation are foregone, due to bounded rationality on the part of employees or limits on the possible complexity of the organization.

In addition, there may be a loss of control by management, as the firm expands its boundaries which was noted by the business historian Chandler (1962, 1982). He observed that as firms grow in size, there is an increasing need to adopt a different organizational structure in order to manage effectively and establish clear strategic objectives. Applying this insight to bancassurance, it may be the case that expanding into insurance increases transaction costs and organizational and managerial complexity so much as to outweigh possible synergy benefits, unless there is an adequate organizational response.

As many managers have found in the 1980s when attempting to reap the benefits of synergy potential of mergers and acquisitions, it is one thing to identify the potential for synergy on paper but quite another to establish actual effects in practice. This section addresses these potential costs of aiming for synergy effects in the context of bancassurance and discusses a possible organizational response.

Porter (1985, p. 331-36) differentiates three possible sources of costs of sharing tangible assets like a branch network for the example of bancassurance. First, there are costs of *co-ordination*. These refer to the fact that sharing common inputs requires a possibly substantial degree of co-ordinating activities, scheduling and re-organising. When sharing a branch network, for example, an insurer and a bank need to agree on common objectives, co-ordinate sales targets and specify product and distribution approach.

Next, Porter identifies the cost of *compromise* as the second main source of costs when sharing tangible inputs. In the context of bancassurance, these costs refer to the fact that branch personnel, for example, can spend less time with selling traditional bank products when the overall number of products is increased. Thus, when insurance products are introduced in addition to the regular product portfolio, it may happen that branch employees are less knowledgeable about the whole product range, since know-how requirements increase. Another example would be the cost of adapting a computer system to the needs of selling insurance. While the basic hardware may be the same, there could be significant adjustment costs adapting the software to include insurance products.[13]

Thirdly, Porter defines the cost of *inflexibility* as a potential barrier which may arise when there is a need to respond to competitors' moves but the strategic relationship between two internal business units reduces the scope of potential responses. As Prahalad and Dos (1992, p. 101-102) note, for example,

> businesses that operate as discrete, stand-alone entities can respond quickly. If they are part of an interdependent set of businesses, then the response time ... is constrained by the managers' ability in that business to convince others of both the need for and the urgency of the change.

In addition, exit barriers may rise if giving up a business unit which is not doing well would imply negative external effects for other related business units. For a full-fledged analysis of synergy effects it is therefore necessary to take account not only of the potential positive effects of entering insurance but also to quantify the potential costs of expanding the bank's line of business in order to be able to determine the overall net synergy effect.[14]

Problems connected to growing firm size can be alleviated to some extent by choosing an adequate organizational structure. Williamson (1975, 1985) builds on Chandler's historical analysis and identifies the "multidivisional" or "M-form" as an organizational structure which economises on transaction costs and therefore allows a firm to grow in size and expand its product portfolio without an accompanying loss in management control.

The M-form is characterised by a decentralised structure consisting of quasi-independent cost and profit centres where divisional managers are responsible for attaining certain sales or performance targets set by company headquarters. As Williamson formulates (1985, p. 283-84):

> the M-form structure removes the general office executives from partisan involvement in the functional parts and assigns operating responsibilities to the division ... A concept of the firm as an internal market thus emerges.

The M-form framework cannot be applied to the case of bancassurance without some adaptation, however. This stems from the fact that an insurance subsidiary cannot be run on a fully divisionalised basis, since this would miss out on possible synergy effects between retail banking and insurance.

In addition, banks have begun to realise that their traditional organizational structure running along product lines does not constitute a satisfactory solution to recognise and serve customer needs. As a result, a number of banks have started to reorganise their internal structure by focusing on different customer groups rather than product lines (e.g. Revell, 1991, Gapper, 1993b).

These two alternative organizational forms are shown in figure 1.12.

An organizational structure according to product lines has the advantage that it pools know-how for a particular product in one department. This may be beneficial where such products are know-how intensive, subject to continuing innovation or requiring a high level of investment in research and development. The main advantage of an organizational form according to customer groups is at the same time the major disadvantage of a product-determined organization: a customer-focused organization is better able to identify customer needs and requirements. In an increasingly competitive environment, banks have come to value the advantage of being closer to the market through a customer-driven organizational structure and more and more banks therefore opt for this internal structure to better serve the needs of the market and thereby try to gain a competitive advantage. In addition, a customer-driven organizational structure supports the allocation of scarce internal resources towards those customer groups which are most profitable for the bank. Recent studies have found that banks do not allocate resources adequately, since there is lack of customer differentiation in retail banking. It is therefore not uncommon to find that banks devote only 20 per cent of their resources to higher-income customers which may account for up to 80 per cent of profits (e.g. Loehneysen *et al.*, 1990). A customer-driven organizational structure helps to prevent such misallocations.

Figure 1.12: Examples of organizational structures according to product lines and customer groups

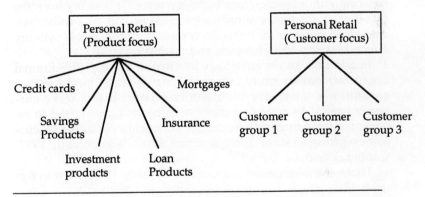

A customer-focused organizational form can also be viewed as a variant of Williamson's M-form where profit responsibility is assigned to customer divisions rather than product units. Such an organizational form also facilitates exploitation of synergy effects and integration of new products such as insurance, since it allows a better focus on customer needs rather than product features. In effect, a customer-focused structure reverses the traditional way of approaching the market, since the first step consists of analysing customer needs and then creating the products to satisfy these needs, rather than creating products first and then approaching customers. In summary, a customer-focused structure therefore helps to economise on transaction costs and allows exploitation of synergy potentials in the area of bancassurance.

6. Conclusions

This first part provided an analysis of the economic incentives for banks to enter the insurance sector. I divided the analysis into industry and firm-level incentives.

Concerning industry-level factors, I discussed the regulatory environment concerning bancassurance, provided a brief analysis of the European banking industry and analysed economic incentives for banks to enter the life insurance sector. The regulatory environment concerning the entry of banks into insurance has changed considerably over the past decade. While regulators have for a long time enforced strict separation between the banking and insurance sectors, more recently they have started to relax these restrictions. Liberalisation was at least partly caused by the fact that few economic arguments support such regulatory separation. While restrictions on insurance production and underwriting remain in force in almost all surveyed countries, distribution of insurance products by banks is now possible in the majority of regulatory regimes. In addition, banks are mostly allowed to acquire or start-up insurance subsidiaries. These provisions have opened the door for banks in most countries wishing to enter the insurance sector. Notable exceptions are Japan and the US where cross-industry entry is still mostly prohibited by regulatory barriers.

A brief analysis of the current state of the banking industry focused on a number of changes which have taken place in the past decade. Increasing internationalisation facilitated by advances in information technology, regulatory liberalisation and increasing disintermediation of large companies have led to a significantly more competitive market in the investment and commercial banking field. In retail banking, on the other hand, the branch is still the dominant channel of distribution despite the fact that banks have started to closely monitor the value-added of each individual branch and shut down those where revenues are not sufficient to cover expenses. At the same time, banks increasingly realise the value of their retail branches which serve as the bridgehead for mostly long-established customer relationships. As branches constitute a high-fixed cost network, however, banks started to explore opportunities to make better use of this sales channel to improve utilisation. It was therefore only a small step to consider introducing insurance products into the traditional banking product portfolio.

Analysing incentives for banks to enter into insurance, I focused on five explanatory factors: demographic changes, the economic environment, savings trends, the tax regime and growth prospects for the industry.

Demographic changes in the Western industrialised countries result from lower birth rates and increased life expectancy which will significantly alter the age pyramid with the number of retired increasing dramatically which need to be supported by a smaller work force.

The economic environment influences the demand for life insurance, since price stability is a necessary prerequisite for a long-term investment such as life insurance and GDP growth rates indicate the relative wealth of the country. Savings rates, on the other hand, constitute the total potential for life insurance. I showed that both savings ratios and insurance rates vary considerably across countries and that life insurance currently has a very different relative significance in Western industrialised countries. While there is likely to be some degree of convergence across countries especially in the European Community with increasing harmonisation, differences are likely to remain pronounced for a considerable period of time to come.

The tax regime also varies across countries with some states providing considerable tax incentives for private retirement provisions. Tax regulations are likely to be one of the most decisive factors in a customer's decision whether to acquire life insurance and the current regime usually favours life insurance over other forms of long-term savings.

Since demand for life insurance is likely to increase further over the next years, growth prospects for the industry are likely to remain substantial. Thus, banks which enter life insurance have the opportunity to participate in this growth trend and share in the considerable profit potential which is associated with life insurance.

The second main area of economic incentives for banks to enter insurance stems from firm-level factors and most especially from possible synergy effects between banking and insurance. Synergies result in a higher return on investment for an integrated firm than for a firm consisting of several stand-alone units. The two most important examples of cost synergies are economies of scale and scope. Scale economies do not provide a significant source of synergies in the context of bancassurance, however, as most effects are exhausted at a relatively small scale. Scope economies, in contrast, provide a much more powerful economic rationale for entering insurance for a bank. They can result from sharing inputs such as the retail distribution network or intangible assets such as a brand name and the established reputation of a bank. Other sources include marketing economies where consumers may prefer to acquire a range of financial products from one source which may result in increased lock-in effects further enforced by switching costs, and diversification advantages since risks of banking and insurance are not fully correlated.

Synergy potentials are significantly greater for life insurance than for general insurance, since distribution economies are much more important for life insurance. I emphasised that striving for synergies also involves possible costs and that it is therefore necessary to determine the net synergy effect of diversification into insurance. Limits to economies of size which arise when a firm gets larger or expands its product portfolio can be successfully overcome by choosing an organizational structure which economises on transaction costs. One such organizational form is the divisionalised structure based on different customer groups.

While I have looked at the question *why* banks enter into insurance in this first part, the following part analyses the issue *how* banks enter the insurance sector.

---

1 Sir Leon Brittan, the EC Commissioner formerly responsible for financial services, recently noted that "our categorisation of financial service activities under the headings 'banking', 'investment services' and 'insurance' is becoming increasingly artificial. As regards products, the vast majority of life policies are best understood simply as savings plans ... As for institutions, we are entering the age of 'Allfinanz' or 'Bancassurance' in which the distinctions between a bank, an investment service house, a leasing company, an insurance company, and so on are breaking down..." (as quoted in OECD, 1992, p. 92).

2 Political observers agreed that one of the major reasons why the US banking reform bill failed in 1991 was pressure which the Association of Independent Insurance Agents placed through lobbying groups on their legislators, since they feared that banks would cut into their market share by being granted greater freedoms of distributing insurance products.

3 See, for example, Merrick and Saunders (1985) and Berlin et al. (1991) on the functioning of deposit insurance schemes. Kareken and Wallace (1978) argue that the deposit insurance scheme is responsible for the large number of bank failures in the US, since it reduces the need for depositors to monitor the prudence of banks and therefore results in a moral hazard problem. See, for example, Jacklin (1987, 89) for an alternative to such deposit insurance schemes.

4 For a more detailed discussion of regulatory issues in financial services see, for example, Baltensperger and Dermine (1992), Goodhart (1989, chapters 8 and 9) and McDowell (1989).

5 In total, 35 banks pursued 40 entry activities into insurance, since some banks entered through more than one entry route.

6 Similar to Ansoff's early definition, Buzzell and Gale (1992, p. 56) define synergy benefits as "those sources of value that allow the business units in a portfolio to achieve higher profitability levels than they would normally achieve as stand-alone operations."

7 See definition 3 of Baumol (1977, p. 811) and definition 2 of Panzar and Willig (1977, p. 484).

8 See Panzar and Willig (1981) for a short account on scope economies and chapters 3 and 4 of Baumol, Panzar and Willig (1982) for a more general treatment.

9 As Gardener (1990, p. 19) notes: "An important objective is to locate the possible existence of shared costs. This is a kind of synergy, working on the interrelationship among different business products in order to create a sustainable advantage over competitors".

10 As Itami (1992, p. 44) notes: "the goal of synergy is to get a free ride. This happens when the resources accumulated in one part of the company are used simultaneously and at no additional expense by other parts".

11 Switching costs in financial services may stem, for example, from the fact that new account numbers need to be communicated to business relations, standing orders need to be re-directed or that bonus payments may be lost for the case of insurance.

12 Consider the following example (Klemperer, 1990): there are two banks located some distance apart in a small town. Both banks first decide on the range of products to be offered and subsequently on the price charged. Two strategies are available to the firms: either to offer the whole (undifferentiated) product line ('supermarket' strategy) or to specialise on particular differentiated products ('specialist' strategy). If both firms

choose the supermarket strategy and they are not differentiated in any other respect (such as qualification of employees, for example), then consumers will maintain relationships with one firm only, as location is the only differing characteristic. If, however, each firm offers a different product range then consumers may maintain relationships with both institutions to reap the benefits of specialisation. If both players choose the specialist strategy, then the incentive to cut prices may be greater than for the supermarket outcome, where more customers are 'locked in' with one of the two identical suppliers and are therefore less sensitive to price movements in single products. Hence, when firms choose specialist strategies the resulting non-cooperative equilibrium may be characterised by lower prices (and profits) than the supermarket outcome, since in the latter case the lock-in effect of customers is stronger.

13 As Porter (1985, p.334) notes, "merging computer systems initially designed for separate financial products has proven difficult, though a system designed to process many products would be effective".

14 Empirical evidence on possible negative net synergy is provided by Grant (1992) who analyses the diversification moves of six large US financial services firms in the 1980s. He concludes that (1992, p.204), "by-and-large, the anticipated benefits have not been forthcoming. The leading diversifiers have, for the most part, shown poor profitability, strategic reversals in several of their diversified businesses, and suspiciously-frequent restructurings and senior management changes." While financial institutions all cited synergy effects as the main strategic rationale for diversifying, in practice, these anticipated synergies turned out to be significantly less than expected, non-existent or even negative. This resulted from several causes (Grant, 1992): first, the desire of customers to benefit from the transaction cost advantage of one-stop shopping was limited and cross-selling rates were much lower than expected. Second, there were considerable difficulties of adapting the indigenous sales channel to distributing new products, since sales personnel needed to be trained in the distribution of new and unfamiliar products and these products often required different skills than those sales personnel were familiar with. Third, there was a considerable degree of 'cultural clash', as financial services such as insurance, retail, commercial and investment banking all breed different organizational cultures which pose problems of compatibility. Finally, there were problems of designing an adequate incentive structure across all levels of the organization which would have encouraged cross-selling and integration of the different kinds of financial services. Interestingly, however, Grant reports that the financial institutions which had moved into insurance performed relatively well in this area as compared to other sectors, outperforming specialist companies (i.e. insurers) in terms of the divisional return on assets.

Chapter Two:
How do Banks Enter Insurance?
Comparative Analysis
of Entry Strategies

This second chapter of the study undertakes a comparative analysis of entry strategies of European banks into insurance, placing the focus of the analysis on the choice of the entry vehicle and examining in the course of the chapter the most important examples of European banks which have entered insurance. The analysis is classified into de novo entries, co-operative distribution alliances, joint ventures and mergers or acquisitions and it focuses on the following key questions:

- Can common patterns be identified which characterise each entry strategy?
- Does the choice of the entry vehicle matter for the overall success of the entry vehicle?
- If so, does any entry vehicle appear to be more successful than its alternatives?
- How can the theoretical and empirical management literature help to explain the relative success of different entry vehicles?
- What other key factors for successfully entering insurance are relevant?

The outline of this chapter is as follows. The first section provides a brief overview of strategic issues in the context of financial services and entry into insurance. Sections two, three, four and five analyse case studies of the four main entry vehicles. Finally, section six analyses key factors for successfully entering insurance in greater detail.

1. Entry strategies into insurance: an overview

1.1. Strategic issues in financial services: the need for a modified approach

The need for a modified analysis of strategic issues in financial services as distinct from physical goods stems from three main sources. First, financial services are intangible in the sense that they do not constitute physical objects, but normally consist of an implicit or explicit contract which specifies particular services to be delivered at a certain time (e.g. Shostak, 1982; Bowen and Schneider, 1988). Financial services are mostly provided in a course of social interaction between the customer and a firm employee (Berry, 1980; Lovelock 1992).[1] Product quality is therefore highly dependent on the abilities and characteristics of the employee who provides the service which results in a lack of product standardization and homogeneity for services in comparison to physical goods.

Second, financial services are frequently long-term relationships between customer and service supplier, characterised by asymmetric information and a fiduciary function of the supplier resulting in a required degree of trust and confidence which the consumer needs to place into the service provider (e.g. Sharpe, 1990). Thus, reputation and reliability of the supplier become crucial buying criteria for the purchaser of a financial service.

Third, unlike in physical goods industries there is no patent protection in financial services and as a result innovative products can be easily copied by competitors. Product differentiation which is a common strategy in physical goods industries, is therefore significantly more difficult in financial services.

As a result of these factors, obtaining a competitive advantage in financial services builds on a modified set of strategic skills and tools than in physical goods industries.

Possibly the most important implication for a financial services firm is the fact that the areas of marketing and organizational behaviour are much closer inter-linked than for a physical goods industry. In the area of marketing the most common approach in the context of physical goods is the well-known marketing mix consisting of the 'four Ps': product, price, place and promotion (e.g. Borden, 1965; McCarthy, 1981).[2] Since financial services usually have a high degree of social interaction, however, a fifth factor, people, is usually included in the marketing mix (e.g. Cowell, 1984). This stems from the fact that the employee is the representative of the organization and it is largely up to her abilities to provide counselling to the customer and to successfully complete the sale.[3] Thus, for a financial services provider it is imperative to place significant emphasis on 'people' which may be its most important organizational asset (Lovelock, 1992b). As a result, it is impossible to maintain a strict separation between the areas of marketing and organizational behaviour.

Strategies of differentiation also differ in their concrete form in financial services from those in physical goods industries. Differentiation requires building up a position which sets the firm apart from its competitors in the customer's perception (Porter, 1980, 1985). Due to the fact that innovative products can be easily copied by competitors, financial services suppliers frequently attempt to build up a reputation for reliability or especially good service quality in order to achieve a lasting strategic advantage (e.g. Reichheld and Sasser, 1990; Howcroft, 1991; Boaden and Gale, 1993).

As a result of these factors, the analysis of strategic issues in financial services requires a modified approach to that of physical goods. The next section deals more specifically with elements of a strategic plan for a bank intending to enter insurance, taking account of the strategic factors which characterise the financial services industry discussed in this section.

1.2. Elements of a strategic plan for a bank entering insurance

Devising an entry strategy into insurance for a bank requires setting up a detailed strategic plan which addresses the main issues of marketing, distribution and organization. Suppose that a bank has decided to enter the insurance sector based on a careful analysis of market opportunities and industry trends, taking into account the economic incentives which were discussed in part one. A strategic entry plan for a bank then needs to comprise the following nine elements:

- *Recognising customer needs:* A thorough analysis of customer needs and requirements needs to be undertaken. This analysis should focus on the specific driving factors which determine consumer behaviour and shed light on the consumer's decision process when purchasing insurance.

• *Market segmentation:* On the basis of the analysis of customer needs, customers should be classified into specific clusters which possess common characteristics and buying behaviour and can be served by similar marketing approaches.

• *Strategic positioning:* The bank needs to determine whether it intends to compete in all market segments or whether it plans to focus on specific segments. In addition, it needs to quantify its strategic objectives in terms of penetrating its customer base and acquiring new customers.

• *Product line:* Based on the careful analysis of customer needs and the intended strategic positioning, the bank needs to determine its product line and its pricing strategy.

• *Promotional strategy:* The bank has to determine how to promote its insurance products and communicate to its customers that it has entered into a new line of business.

• *Information technology support:* The bank needs to adapt its information and processing systems towards selling insurance products. This includes support for sales staff in the form of databases and expert systems, for example, as well as sales monitoring systems and processing facilities.

• *Distribution:* The bank needs to decide on its distributional approach, such as determining whether insurance products should be sold by insurance specialists or through bank branch staff.

• *Training of employees:* Depending on the particular distribution approach chosen, the bank needs to train its employees in the sales techniques of insurance products.

• *Incentive structure:* The bank needs to devise an incentive structure which optimally motivates its employees to actively sell insurance products.

All of these issues are mutually dependent and need to be considerd in their totality as well as their interaction. It needs to be insured that all elements are mutually consistent and fit together to form a coherent entry strategy.

Possibly, one of the most significant strategic decisions in the context of entering insurance is the choice of the entry vehicle. In general, banks face four major entry vehicles when entering insurance which are de novo entry, joint venture, distribution alliance and merger or acquisition, as illustrated in figure 2.1.

Figure 2.1: Alternative entry vehicles for banks entering insurance

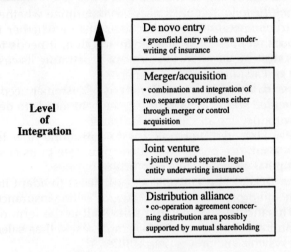

Level of Integration

De novo entry
• greenfield entry with own underwriting of insurance

Merger/acquisition
• combination and integration of two separate corporations either through merger or control acquisition

Joint venture
• jointly owned separate legal entity underwriting insurance

Distribution alliance
• co-operation agreement concerning distribution area possibly supported by mutual shareholding

There is a mutual dependence of the elements of the strategic entry plan and the choice of the entry vehicle. Consider, for example, the question of training employees in insurance know-how. If the bank chooses de novo entry then training programmes need to be devised independently, while in a joint venture or a strategic alliance training can be devised in co-operation with the insurance partner. Similarly, promotional strategy and product line are influenced by the decision which entry vehicle is chosen.

The following sections will discuss each of these four major entry vehicles and examine the most important case studies for each entry route.

1.3 The chosen research approach to the case studies

In order to select the following compilation of case studies, I compiled a comprehensive database of entry moves of the 60 largest EC banks already discussed in part one.

I decided to focus on the four countries France, Germany, the UK and the Netherlands where the entry of banks into the insurance sector has been most prolific. Whenever the phenomenon of bancassurance is discussed, references are usually made to one of these four countries. Analysing the database of 35 overall entry moves shows that 25 entry moves took place in these four countries. The final sample covers 18 of these entry moves undertaken by the 13 institutions which are described in the following case studies.[4]

Cases selected include the six largest UK banks, the three large German 'Grossbanken' and the two largest French and Dutch banks.

In order to collect information on these cases, I derived data from three sources:

- annual reports and company statements;
- industry reports and newspaper and journal cuttings;
- company interviews with managers concerned with the strategic implementation of entry into insurance;

In addition, I undertook some branch visits to familiarise myself with product line and basic selling approach.

Industry reports include publications by Salomon Brothers (1990), Lafferty Publications (1990) and Arthur Andersen (1990).

In order to structure the analysis of the case studies a comparative structure of presentation is chosen. This enables the reader to juxtapose specific aspects and sub-topics more easily across different cases. The following sub-topics are dealt with for each case:

- Background information on the firm(s) involved;
- Reasons for entering bancassurance and choice of entry vehicle;
- Marketing and distribution approach to bancassurance;
- Incentive structure;
- Assessment of success of entry into bancassurance.

The amount of available information differs between cases. This stems from the fact that not all firms were willing to reveal all relevant data. I decided to include all relevant information which officials disclosed for each case, rather than attempting to artificially standardise the case format which would not do full justice to the case under scrutiny. As a result, the case studies differ somewhat in length.

The case studies are presented according to the type of the entry vehicle rather than the main operating country, as it became apparent in the course of the research that some of the characteristics and problems are very similar for the same entry vehicle. Success of entry seems to be determined more by the choice of the entry vehicle rather than by the operating country which can be well-illustrated by the fact that highly successful institutions in the area of bancassurance exist in the same country side-by-side with not-very-sucessful banks which have chosen a different entry vehicle. Highly successful institutions have therefore a lot more in common with other successful firms in a different country than with a less-successful firm in the same country. The analytical section succeeding the case studies will discuss this issue in much greater detail.

Table 2.1 provides an overview of the case studies discussed in the next sections and gives the year of the entry in brackets.

Table 2.1: Overview of case studies

De novo entry	Distribution alliance	Joint venture	Merger or acquisition
• TSB (1967) • Crédit Agricole (1986) • Deutsche Bank (1989) • Barclays Bank (1969)	• BNP/UAP (1989) • Dresdner Bank and Allianz (1989) • Bank of Scotland and Standard Life (1989)	• Royal Bank of Scotland and Scottish Equitable (1990) • Commerzbank and DBV (1990) • Midland Bank and Commercial Union (1987)	• NMB Postbank and Nationale Nederlanden (1991) • Lloyds Bank and Abbey Life (1988) • Rabobank and Interpolis (1990)

2. De novo entry: starting from scratch

De novo entry is not normally a common form of entry in retail financial services. This stems from the fact that it is frequently argued that building up a customer franchise is such a time-consuming process that it is virtually impossible to enter retail financial services from scratch. As a result, cross-border entry moves in retail financial services almost always take the form of acquisitions of indigenous institutions rather than setting up a subsidiary from scratch (e.g. Casson, 1990).

However, the situation of banks' entry into insurance is different, since banks already possess a customer franchise which is the asset most difficult to build up from scratch. Thus, the question whether de novo entry is a suitable form of entry for the bank into insurance depends on a range of operational issues. The following sections analyse four case studies of de novo entry of banks in the UK, Germany and France.

2.1. TSB: setting a precedence in European bancassurance

2.1.1. Background information on the bank

Trustee Savings Bank (TSB) Group, the amalgamation of the UK savings banks, is the fifth-largest UK bank with a capital of ECU 2.7 billion and pre-tax profits of ECU 3.4 million in 1991. In 1992 it has a total branch network of around 1,400 and 37,000 employees. In total, TSB serves around 7 million customers.

In 1989 TSB started with a significant organisational restructuring programme which aimed at reducing costs, streamlining and redesigning the branch network. The number of regional units was reduced and back office functions were taken out of the majority of branches and centralised in customer service centres. This allows branch personnel to spend significantly more time with the customer in the sales process. Finally, branch design was altered to open plan offices. More than 5,000 staff were shed in the retail division in the course of the cost reduction programme.

2.1.2. Reasons for entering insurance and choice of entry vehicle

TSB was the second bank in the UK setting up a de novo life insurance subsidiary in 1967, one year after Lloyds Bank. Thus, TSB has owned a unit trust and life insurance subsidiary ever since it was founded. Entry into insurance took place because it was perceived to promise significant profit potential.

Two insurance acquisitions turned out to be failures resulting in subsequent divestments. In 1987 Hill House Hammond was acquired, a retail broker chain focusing on motor and home insurance. It was sold off in 1991 for ECU 38 million after lack of success. Target Life which was also acquired in 1987 and focused on selling unit-linked life and pension products through independent financial advisers, tied agents and a small direct sales force was later sold off to Equity&Law after an unsatisfactory performance.

TSB offers not only life and pension products but also general coverage such as home, contents, motor, travel and credit insurance. It underwrites all products except motor and commercial insurance.

2.1.3. Marketing and distribution approach to bancassurance

TSB Group was for a long time organisationally separated into two profit centres, TSB Trust (Insurance) and TSB Bank. This separation was kept throughout all lines of business with some limited co-operation in product development, specifically in the area of linked investment products with insurance coverage attached. In 1992 TSB re-organised its retail financial services division in order to adopt a more customer-focused structure, similar to that illustrated in figure 1.12 in part one. Banking and insurance activities were integrated at top management level at headquarters. The objective of such integration is to adopt a customer-focused organisational structure rather than a product or sector-oriented approach. As a company official notes in a personal interview:

> management perceived that since the personal customer is the focus of our sales and marketing efforts, it does not make sense to maintain two separate divisions which are concerned with selling retail insurance and banking products. Therefore, we decided to streamline our organisation in such a way as to unify sales and marketing responsibilities for the retail sector in one organisational unit all the way down to the individual branch.

The organisational structure of branches is such that there is a branch manager who is responsible for the administrative functioning of the branch and a sales and marketing manager who co-ordinates the sales efforts and is responsible for meeting specific sales targets. Branch and sales manager have equal standing and co-operate closely in the running of the day-to-day business of the branch.

TSB initially experimented with selling life and pension products through branch staff and continues to do so today for simple standardised general insurance products such as motor, household and fire. In the life sector, however, this distribution approach was soon changed, as it turned out that the training requirements for branch personnel were significant and that it was too cumbersome for branch personnel to keep up to date with new products, changing legislation, taxation rules and specific regulations concerning life and pension products. In addition, the areas of life and pension products require a substantial degree of individual financial counselling which turned out to be too time-consuming when provided by retail banking staff.

Instead of training branch banking employees to sell life insurance, TSB management decided instead to engage in a novel distribution approach. Branch personnel identifies potential life insurance customers who have either expressed an interest or are likely candidates for acquiring life insurance. Branch personnel systematically analyses its customer franchise with the help of a specifically designed database according to a number of criteria such as age, financial status and other insurance coverage to identify potential selling leads. The branch manager then writes to the customer who was identified in this way, suggests a particular product and requests an appointment with a TSB insurance specialist. These insurance specialists which are especially trained to advice customers on life products serve one to three branches each. Around 850 insurance specialists therefore 'travel' between their assigned branches to hold appointments with customers at these branches. In addition, they also visit customers outside regular branch opening hours to achieve maximum flexibility and convenience for customers. After the branch manager has 'paved the way', the insurance consultant proceeds to contact the prospective customer and suggests an appointment during the allotted time period when he or she is visiting the nearest branch. The insurance specialist then offers a comprehensive financial analysis to the customer to determine the optimal life product which best suits the needs of the customer.

In addition to these insurance specialists, TSB maintains a direct sales force of more than 200 agents which is responsible for direct marketing initiatives as well as those customers who do not frequently visit their branch.

TSB has segmented its customer base and identified five customer groups which are primarily stratified according to age group. For each segment it has analysed the main financial needs and has structured its product range in order to be able to satisfy these needs.

2.1.4. Incentive structure

In order to ensure close co-operation between insurance specialist and branch personnel, specialists spend a significant amount of time in the branches to gain trust and confidence of the branch's employees. They have a natural incentive to co-operate with branch personnel, since their sales performance depends crucially on receiving 'sales leads' from branch employees. Insurance specialists are paid on a salary basis, but can double their salary with commissions. While branch personnel does not receive a commission for passing on successful 'warm leads' to insurance specialists, both branch employees and insurance specialists are part of the same organisational unit and are assessed according to specified targets.

2.1.5. Success of entry

TSB's entry into insurance has been highly successful. Today, the bank has the second-highest market share in unit-linked and pension products in the UK. Its insurance specialists sell around 25 to 30 contracts per month compared to an industry average of only 6 to 9 contracts. Productivity is thus four to five times the level of the industry average.

As is apparent from table 2.2, TSB Insurance contributes around 30 per cent to total profits of the retail financial services division and is thereby the most successful life operation of a bank in Europe, together with Crédit Agricole's Prédica which the next section discusses. TSB's profits from insurance have grown by a compound annual growth rate of 27 per cent between 1989 to 1992. In 1992, 74 per cent of total insurance profits of ECU 170 million originated from life and pension products, 23 per cent derived from general insurance, while 2 per cent originated from unit trust business. Total premiums in 1992 were ECU 170 million in life and pension products and ECU 217 million in general insurance. Total assets of life and pension funds equalled ECU 3.5 billion in 1992.

Total group profits of TSB, as listed in the fourth column of table 2.2 have been affected by losses of its investment banking subsidiary Hill Samuel which had to provide significant bad debt provisions. Total provisions for bad and doubtful debts amounted to ECU 790 million in 1992 after a charge of ECU 860 million in 1991.

Table 2.2: Contribution of TSB's insurance business to total profits from retail financial services

	Profits from insurance division (ECU million)	As percentage of profits from retail financial services	Total group operating profits (ECU million)
1989	82	30 %	440
1990	115	28 %	430
1991	158	30 %	0
1992	170	30 %	140

Source: Annual reports.

Management still perceives significant growth opportunities for selling insurance products to its retail banking customers. It estimates that out of a total pool of 4 to 5 million customers who are potential customers for buying life insurance, only slightly more than one million have actually acquired life insurance from TSB Insurance.

2.2. Crédit Agricole's Prédica

2.2.1. Background information on the bank

Caisse National de Crédit Agricole (CNCA) is the central organisational unit of the French co-operative banks and is owned by the almost 3,000 local banks. It is not only the largest French bank, but also the largest European bank with a capital of ECU 13 billion and pre-tax profits of ECU 1.4 billion in 1991. It has a vast retail network of 8,421 branches in 1991 and a massive customer base of 17 million. Every third current account in France is actually with a branch of Crédit Agricole and its domestic market share for loans is almost 20 per cent.

2.2.2. Reasons for entering insurance and choice of entry vehicle

In 1985 Crédit Agricole founded a wholly owned life insurance subsidiary, Prédica, and introduced the first products in

September 1986. The decision to move into insurance was motivated to a significant extent by the increasing share which insurers were taking of total savings in France, a phenomenon already discussed in part one. Since banks were therefore losing their cheap funding base of retail deposits, management perceived a need to reverse this trend by offering insurance products as well. The product range of Prédica is therefore targeted at savings products linked to life insurance such as the *bon de capitalisation*. These products have a tax advantage compared to simple savings deposits and have chiefly contributed to the erosion of French banks' retail deposit base. In addition, as a company official notes in an interview, "insurance is an activity which is close in approach and characterstics to those of banking" and can therefore be integrated into the banking environment.

De novo entry was chosen as an entry vehicle because it was considered to best suit the bank's operating environment and provide the best opportunity to tailor a specific product strategy for the bank which takes account of the fact that the branch rather than an agency network is the main distribution channel. Thus, the product line is kept simple, as the next section discusses.

Insurance plays a significant role in the group's strategy. As a company official notes in an interview, "insurance is one of our principal strategic priorities in the CA group for the years to come ... our objective with the time horizon of the year 2,000 is to be as much of an insurer as a bank".

2.2.3. *Marketing and distribution approach to bancassurance*

Prédica focuses on relatively simple products which have a substantial savings element and are therefore easy to comprehend and to explain by bank staff. Products include term and whole life, pensions and retirement as well as savings plans with risk coverage, thus covering the most essential needs of customers. As a company official notes, management decided that the number of life products shall not exceed the maximum number of ten and the actual number of products offered is actually less than ten. This not only significantly speeds up the training process of bank employees, but also facilitates the identification process of front-line sales personnel with the new products, since the product range remains manageable.[5] In terms of product positioning both internally and externally, Prédica thus ensured that the new products are actually perceived as "bank" products with an insurance element attached, rather than insurance products sold by a bank. As a company official notes, such positioning is aimed to minimise the 'cultural' problems which may occur during the introductory phase of insurance products into a banking environment.

Prédica offers significantly better terms than the standard insurers. It can afford to do so without cutting the profit margin, as distribution costs are significantly lower than for insurance companies. This results from employing the branch network as the sole distribution channel at low marginal costs. Thus, the synergy effects which part one discussed can be fully exploited. Crédit Agricole launched a comprehensive advertising campaign in the mass media to promote its products and pursues an ambitious sales programme in the branches.

In its communication strategy Prédica focuses on the tax savings which are associated with its life insurance products. Under the advertising slogan *Faites fondre vos impots et fleurir votre epargne* (Reduce your taxes and flourish your savings) it introduces its products which are tax-advantaged.

2.2.4. Incentive structure

Prédica employs salaried personnel in the branches which do not receive commissions. Training of branch employees is focused on a select group of employees of around 9,000 by 1993 which have acquired the more specialised know-how required for selling insurance products and which passed internal examinations to qualify as insurance agents. While a small bonus is paid to these employees, they continue to be compensated primarily on a salary basis to reduce problems of having two different reward systems side by side in the branch which may create animosity and lack of co-operation between the personnel concerned.

In addition, branches are given targets for selling insurance-related products and these are taken into account in the branch manager's overall assessment.

2.2.5. Success of entry

Already in its first year of full operation Prédica managed to attain a market share of new premiums for simple life insurance of

21 percent. By 1989 it had the second-largest overall market share with 11 per cent in the French market, closely following the market leader UAP which had a market share of 12 per cent.

By the end of 1992, Prédica had 4.8 million policyholders in France and a premium volume of ECU 2.7 billion. Central head-quarters has a very lean management structure with only 150 employees in 1992. This enables it to keep its cost level down and achieve a high level of efficiency. As illustrated in figure 2.2, profits before tax of Prédica increased significantly between 1988 and 1992 with a compound annual growth rate of 36 per cent.

Figure 2.2: Development of Prédica's profits before tax from 1988 to 1992

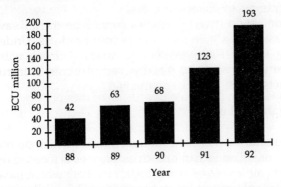

Source: Annual reports of Prédica.

In summary, Crédit Agricole's entry into life insurance has been most successful so far and the bank currently attempts to repeat this success story in the area of general insurance. Thus, in 1991 Crédit Agricole entered property and casualty insurance through founding a new subsidiary, Pacifica. Similarly to Prédica, it uses Crédit Agricole's bank branches as its main distribution channel and sales are undertaken through specially trained branch employees. The product range so far includes simple personal motor and home insurance but sales have been comparatively slow up to the present and do not compare to the dramatic success of Prédica. This underlines the lower synergy potential between general insurance and bank products which I discussed in part one of the study.

2.3. Deutsche Bank's Lebensversicherung

2.3.1. Background information on the bank

Deutsche Bank (DB) is the largest and most profitable German bank with a capital of ECU 10 billion and pre-tax profits of ECU 2 billion in 1991 and around 1,700 domestic branches. DB is a prime example of the German type of a universal bank which is active in all areas of banking ranging from retail business over corporate banking to international wholesale activities. It is the biggest retail bank in Germany accounting for the greatest share of savings deposits and mortgages. Nevertheless, due to the significant role played by the savings and co-operative banks in Germany, DB only has a market share of about 5 per cent in retail banking.

2.3.2. Reasons for entering insurance and choice of entry vehicle

DB was the first German bank to enter life insurance on a significant scale by founding Lebensversicherung der Deutschen Bank AG (DB Leben) which went on the market in September 1989. Before entering life insurance on a full scale, it had only offered a savings product with insurance coverage. However, this product was not granted the tax advantages which are associated with standard life insurance products in Germany despite the fact that it is similar in its product characteristics to a life policy. As a bank official notes in a personal interview, the responsible regulatory authorities did not grant tax-favoured status to this bank product at least partly due to pressure from the life insurance industry which feared the increased competition from banks cutting into their market share. Such entry-deterring behaviour on the part of the insurance industry was not successful, however, as DB decided to set up a life subsidiary to attack the insurance market directly. This decision drew an angry response from Allianz, Germany's market leader and Europe's largest insurer which threatened to terminate all business relations with DB if the bank went ahead with its plans to attack the profitable life insurance market, a considerable threat considering Allianz' massive investment portfolio. DB, however, was unperturbed and Allianz responded by shifting business to Deutsche's main rival Dresdner Bank (see below).

The main reason for DB to enter life insurance was the increasing share which this form of insurance gained in total personal savings of retail customers. As an executive of DB notes: "it was ... high time for banks to reassert their position in private asset formation by offering their own life insurance products" (Pauluhn, 1991, p. 22).

DB's management excluded joint ventures and strategic alliances as possible entry forms into insurance. This aversion against co-operative arrangements reflects a general strategic view of DB management which believes that such ventures are riddled with problems and unlikely to be successful. As Deutsche Bank's chief executive formulates: "according to our experiences, there is little inclination to co-operate closely in multilateral alliances" (Kopper, 1990, p. 69, author's translation). Specifically for the case of bancassurance, a DB executive (Pauluhn, 1991, p. 22) notes that:

> Co-operation creates a major problem in sales, namely that two large companies with different corporate cultures are in effect brought into collision on the issue of financial provision for the customer's future.

Excluding the possibility of a strategic alliance or a distribution agreement, management was faced with a choice to set up a new subsidiary from scratch or to acquire a life insurer. Its decision to favour de novo entry was motivated by a number of reasons. Most importantly, DB aimed to start up with a bank-tailored strategy, rather than taking over an insurance organisation with its associated sales culture and established product range which would then have to be re-directed to fit Deutsche Bank's requirements and strategic goals. In addition, DB management believed that possible 'cultural' problems when blending an insurance sales organisation into the retail banking environment would make successful entry more difficult. As a company official notes in a personal interview, "management believed that identification of branch employees with the new life products would be greater if entry was an indigenous development rather than acquisition".

Despite these considerations, in 1992 Deutsche Bank acquired a 65 per cent stake in Deutscher Herold Holding, an insurer with subsidiaries in both life and non-life business. In 1992 this insurer had capital and reserves of ECU 235 million and achieved profits in life insurance of ECU 14 million and in non-life insurance of ECU 13 million. Deutsche's strategic motivation to acquire the insurer was to gain an additional distribution outlet for its banking products through Herold's sales force and, in addition, to enter the area of non-life insurance by drawing on Herold's accumulated expertise in this area.

2.3.3. Marketing and distribution approach to bancassurance

Deutsche Bank focuses on simple packaged life products which can be sold through the branch network without the need to invest a significant amount of time into training bank employees. It aims to offer only a selective range of insurance products, as an executive explains: "To be really successful, even a universal bank must be highly selective in the additional services it decides to offer. It would be a serious mistake for banks to be swept away by the ambition to offer every kind of service..." (Pauluhn, 1991, p. 21). According to this executive, this stems primarily from the fact that there are limits to the number of products which a customer adviser in a branch can explain and sell with confidence.

In order to differentiate its products from those of the standard life insurers, DB introduced three innovative characteristics of its life products. These are actively communicated in the bank's product information and advertising to make the differentiating characteristics explicit to the customer. Firstly, the commission which is paid to branches is amortised over a number of years in the premium payments of the customer rather than only in the first and second year after the sale, as is common with standard life insurance. This has tangible price advantages for the customer who leaves the contract before actual expiration. In addition, a higher amount of premiums is invested in the first two years, resulting in a better net present value for the policy holder. Secondly, part of the accumulated interest which is usually paid out at the end of the contract is deducted from premiums from the first year of the policy onwards which leads to an overall reduction of premiums for the customer. Finally, the customer is informed on an annual basis about accumulated premiums and actual coverage, resulting in greater transparency for the policy holder than is normal practice in German life insurance.

In terms of advertising, DB follows an aggressive strategy with regular commercials in the mass media, stressing the solidity of the Deutsche Bank brand name. Its advertising theme is *"Durch die Bank gut versichert"* ("Well-insured by the bank").

It has carefully segmented its customer franchise and specifically targets professionals, small business owners and employees in its advertising communication.

After the acquisition of Deutscher Herold, DB intends to change its distribution approach, however. It is planned that insurance specialists are to be stationed in branches so as to provide more expert advice to customers than regular branch personnel can deliver. This is somewhat similar to TSB's development in terms of its distribution approach which started out by selling life insurance through its regular branch personnel, but soon realised that expert advice is needed to fully penetrate the intricacies of life insurance products. A DB official notes that regular branch staff already has to be familiar with around 60 banking products. Adding another 10 or more life and non-life insurance products would exceed the limit of what seems manageable. Thus, insurance experts shall take over from bank personnel to deal with insurance sales.[6]

2.3.4. Incentive structure

Individual branches as a whole receive a credit for any life policy sold, while employees do not participate in commissions. According to a bank official, this lack of commissions for frontline sales personnel has the advantage that it ensures that the customer receives the product which most adequately satisfies her needs, rather than a product which offers the highest commission level. Thus, the quality of advice is likely to be less biased and more objective than that of insurance sales personnel. This is documented by the fact that the share of term life compared to whole life products is significantly greater for Deutsche Bank than for life insurers which reward their sales personnel with a significantly greater commission level for whole life products. In 1991 the share of whole life of total insurance premiums was 57 per cent which compares to an industry average of 80 per cent.

Table 2.3: Summary statistics for Deutsche Bank Lebens-versicherung

in ECU

	Volume of new policies	Total number of contracts	Premium revenue	Profit/Loss
1990	3.6 billion	94,000	125 mill.	-13 mill.
1991	4.1 billion	158,000	300 mill.	-8 mill.
1992	5.6 billion	217,000	335 mill.	-1 mill.
CAGR	+16%	+32%	+61%	n.a.

n.a. not applicable
CAGR: Compound Annual Growth Rate
Source: Annual Reports DB Leben.

2.3.5. Success of entry

DB Leben has achieved substantial growth rates since its start of business. Only six months after its inception, Deutsche Bank sold on average 10,000 life policies per month. The fact that the start-up has almost reached break-even in its third full year of operation is noted with some satisfaction by DB executives who cite a statement by the former CEO of Allianz who commented on DB's entry into life insurance that it takes at least ten years for a life insurance start-up to reach profitability. In 1993 DB Leben is among the largest 15 life insurers in terms of new business. Table 2.3 depicts some financial data for DB Leben for the years 1990 to 1992.

It remains to be seen whether Deutsche Bank's entry into non-life business will be equally successful as its entry into the life insurance sector.

2.4. Barclays Bank

2.4.1. Background information on the bank

Barclays Bank, the largest UK bank with a capital of ECU 7.6 billion and a pre-tax loss of ECU 320 million in 1992 has almost 2,300 UK branches and 48,000 employees in UK retail banking. The Barclays Bank Group has 13 million personal customers and the domestic bank has 6.2 million customers (excluding Barclaycard customers). It is active in all areas of retail, commercial and investment banking and is therefore practically a universal bank. Most recently, Barclays suffered significant loan losses and bad debt provisions for such lending activities amounting to a record ECU 3.3 billion in 1992, resulting in the first corporate loss in the bank's history.

2.4.2. Reasons for entering insurance and choice of entry vehicle

Barclays Bank has been active in the life insurance market since 1969 when it acquired Martins Bank which in turn had acquired Unicorn Securities in 1963 with its subsidiary Griffin Assurance. A major strategic change occured in 1988 when Barclays was faced with the decision to polarise in-house or tie with an independent supplier under the Financial Services Act. The decision to continue to employ in-house suppliers was based on the perceived strength of the expertise which had already been built up through Barclays Life Assurance and its unit-trust subsidiary Unicorn. At the same time, it decided to establish a small independent brokerage firm, Barclays Insurance Service Company (Bisco) which acts an IFA for those customers who prefer independent advice.

2.4.3. Marketing and distribution approach to bancassurance

Barclays Life Assurance has a sales force of 1,525 in 1993, up from 900 in 1989. This sales force is planned to be increased further to around 2,000 in the near future. The distribution approach of Barclays Life focuses on this commissioned sales force which provides more than 90 per cent of total sales. An estimated 80 per cent of sales result from 'warm leads' by branches, a system similar to that of TSB. This system of branch referals was established only in 1988. Sales agents are associated with one or two branches and work in close co-operation with branch employees.

In terms of its marketing approach, Barclays has an extensive database which allows stratification of customers according to personalised rather than account-based data including criteria such as age, family status and income. As a company official notes in a personal interview, "in insurance, we could certainly not rely on business which walks in the door. For a proactive sales approach, the identification of sales leads such as insufficient insurance coverage, for example, is the key factor of success". The systematic analysis of its vast customer database is therefore the basis of Barclays' sales approach.

2.4.4. Incentive structure

Branch employees do not receive any commission for passing on sales leads to sales agents. Sales agents currently work on a commission basis with only a small base salary. However, this payment system is supposed to be changed by the end of 1994 to a salary-dominated payment structure with an attached bonus paid out according to performance. As a company official explains in a personal interview, this change in incentive structures stems from the strategic objective to relieve agents from the pressure to "make a sale in all circumstances". In addition, the company expects that regulatory pressures are likely to lead to a move away from the commission-only payment structure. It also hopes to exploit its new payment structure as positioning sales agents in a more favourable light as counsellors rather than "hard sellers", similarly to Deutsche Bank's selling approach.

2.4.5. Success of entry

Barclays has achieved significant growth in particular with its unit-linked products. In 1992 Barclays Financial Services (BFS) which comprises life assurance, general brokerage and investment services achieved a profit of ECU 244 million, a CAGR of 15 per cent since 1987. New regular premiums in life insurance almost doubled from slightly more than ECU 66 million in 1988 to almost ECU 130 million in 1992, with ECU 42 million in pensions and ECU 84 million in life insurance. Single premiums in 1992 amounted to ECU 7 million in life insurance and ECU 93 million in pensions. As is shown in table 2.4, profits from insurance constitute an increasing proportion of total group profits. While group profits have steadily fallen over the last years with a loss of ECU 320 million reported in 1992, profits from Barclays Financial Services have consistently improved until 1991. In 1992 profits from life insurance decreased for the first time by ECU 20 million which stemmed from reduced sales. While this may indicate that a profit plateau has been reached, the overall profit surge since entering life insurance demonstrates the success of a strategy of diversification into insurance which is less affected by economic downturns than retail banking and especially lending activities.

Table 2.4: Profits of Barclays' Financial Services Division from 1987 to 1992

	Profits of Barclays Financial Services (ECU mill.)	Profits before taxation of Barclays (ECU mill.)	as % of group profits
1987	113	446	25%
1988	137	1,830	7%
1989	217	830	24%
1990	240	1,187	24%
1991	281	701	40%
1992	265	(320)	n.a.

n.a.: not applicable
Source: Annual reports.

Barclays' management still perceives significant growth potential for its insurance business. A company official notes that with around 1 million policyholders, currently only around 7-8 per cent of its total potential customer base contract with BFS. Thus, more than 90 per cent of the market are still untapped and there is significant scope for expansion.[7]

2.5. Comparative summary of de novo entry case studies

Table 2.5 provides a summary of the key variables for the four case studies under scrutiny. It becomes apparent that all banks have chosen a different approach to enter insurance. For example, while Crédit Agricole distributes life products through non-commissioned branch staff, Barclays and TSB have chosen to introduce insurance specialists into the branch. While TSB staff is primarily salary-based, Barclays currently still has a predominantly commission-based structure. It is also apparent, however, that all de novo entry strategies have been very successful.

Table 2.5: Summary table of de novo entry case studies

	TSB	Crédit Agricole	Deutsche Bank	Barclays Bank
Background	Fifth-largest UK bank, publicly quoted, lower profits recently due to losses in investment banking	Largest French bank, co-operative ownership, very profitable	Largest German bank, publicly quoted, very profitable	Largest UK bank, publicly quoted, lower profits recently due to high bad debt write-offs
Year and reason for entering insurance	1967; perceived profit potential due to synergy effects between banking and insurance	1985; mainly defensive move as life insurers were increasing share of total savings	1989; mainly defensive move similar to Credit Agricole	1969; synergy effects in asset management and distribution
Distribution approach	Insurance specialists based in branches	Sales through regular branch staff	Currently sales through regular branch staff, but changes planned	Insurance specialists based in branches
Incentive structure	Salary but commissions can double income for insurance specialists. No commissions for branch staff	Salary with only small bonus	Salary only	Insurance specialists primarily commission-based. No commissions for branch staff
Success of entry	Highly successful. Insurance profits contribute around 30 per cent of retail financial services profits	Highly successful. Insurance contributes around 15 per cent of total group profits	Relatively successful. Only four years after start-up belongs already to 15 largest life insurers in Germany.	Very successful. Insurance contributed on average for 25 per cent of group profits over last five years.

3. Co-operative distribution alliances: linking distribution channels

A strategic distribution alliance between a bank and an insurer may take the form of a reciprocal or unilateral distribution agreement between the co-operating firms by employing the respective indigenous distribution channel. Thus, a bank may include insurance products in its product portfolio which it distributes through its branch network. In return, it may attempt to distribute its own bank products through the sales network of the insurer. For each product sold through the distribution channel of the co-operating firm, a commission is usually paid. This provides the sales incentive to actively push the products of the partner. At the same time, it provides a stimulus to the originator of the product to supply the partner with training and selling expertise.

Williamson (1975) notes that co-operative ventures are intermediate organizational forms positioned between market exchange and internal firm transaction. They are organizational hybrids where two firms need to share some common objectives but do not merge.

The following section analyses three examples of co-operative distribution alliances between banks and insurers in France, Germany and the UK.

3.1. BNP and UAP

3.1.1. Background information on the bank and insurer

Banque National de Paris (BNP) is the third-largest French bank with a total capital of ECU 9 billion and pre-tax profits of ECU 763 million in 1991. BNP, which was privatised in 1993, has a network of offices of 2,600 in France and 41,000 employees in 1991.

UAP, which is still state-owned, is the largest French insurer with a capital of ECU 6.8 billion in 1991. It has the largest market share in the life insurance market with 12 per cent in 1989 and total premiums of ECU 3.5 billion. In the non-life sector it is the third-largest insurer with a market share of 10 per cent and premiums of ECU 2.4 billion in 1989. It has a total customer base of around 6 million policyholders.

3.1.2. Reasons for entering bancassurance and choice of entry vehicle

In April 1989 the two companies entered an equity swap where each firm took a 10 percent stake in the other company. This cross-shareholding was increased to 20 per cent in 1991. On a financial level, this transaction was primarily aimed at helping BNP to meet the capital adequacy guidelines of the Bank for International Settlements with UAP taking over securitised assets of BNP. On a strategic level, entry into insurance was aimed to assist diversification of revenues. As a company official notes in an interview: "Insurance today constitutes a major pillar of diversification ... insurance is aimed to account for 15 to 20 per cent of group results by the end of the decade".

On an operational level, a distribution alliance was established where BNP distributes non-life insurance products of UAP and the insurer distributes credit products of BNP. The focus on non-life products results from the fact that BNP founded its own life subsidiary, Natio Vie, in 1985. This de novo entry was highly successful with significant growth rates since inception. In 1991 Natio Vie had a capital of ECU 55 million, total revenues of ECU 800 million compared to ECU 37 million in 1985 and a net operating income of ECU 32 million compared to ECU 16 million in 1988. Net operating income in 1991 constituted 3 per cent of consolidated net operating income of BNP France. Natio Vie had a total of 580,000 customers in 1991, thereby occupying the ninth position in the French life insurance market in terms of new premiums. Natio Vie has stationed around 2,000 insurance specialists in the branches of BNP who co-operate with branch employees to sell life products. Similarly to Prédica, Natio Vie has been particularly successful with tax-favoured savings products such as the *bon de capitalisation* and the *plans d'épargne populaires*.

In the non-life sector, however, BNP management perceived the need to establish a link with an experienced insurer, since the area of risk assessment and the calculation of actuarially correct premiums requires know-how which was thought to be difficult to built up via greenfield entry.

Asked about the reason for the choice of the entry vehicle, a company official notes in an interview that

> BNP did not welcome to engage itself in an area -non-life insurance- which is not on its traditional home turf. The alliance with UAP presents the advantage of combining the know-how of a big insurer (technical management of contracts, management of claims handling) with the distribution capacity of BNP retail branch network ... One can see well what a true alliance can bring to each of the two partners: for the insurer it provides access to a substantial sales network for financial products, for the banker it implies an enlargement of its product line, for both parties it entails additional revenues without having

to make investments except training its sales force (Lebegue, 1993, author's translation).

While these reasons seem convincing in theory, in practice there are significant implementation problems, as becomes apparent in the next sections.

3.1.3. Marketing, distribution approach, incentive structure and success of entry

Starting in 1989, the distribution alliance in the non-life sector was tested in five regional areas where each firm distributed a range of basic products of the other company. These products included standardised motor, household and complimentary health insurance. On the banking side, products included consumer loans and mortgages.

However, results of the co-operation in the test areas were considered to be clearly disappointing. In the five regional test areas, only around 1,500 insurance contracts were sold by the 12 participating bank employees in the trial period 1990, a level falling short by 3 to 4 times of profitability. The 30 participating sales agents of UAP, on the other hand, arranged only 100 loans for BNP.

These disappointing results can be explained by lack of incentives on both sides of the alliance. On the banking side, the incentive to sell non-life insurance products is reduced by the relatively low margins in this sector. In addition, cost effectiveness was hampered by the long duration of counselling given to the customer, substantially exceeding that of an insurance agent. Furthermore, bank employees had to acquaint themselves with unfamiliar products which, unlike life policies, are quite different from traditional banking products.

On the insurance side, on the other hand, there were considerable 'cultural' problems selling BNP products on the part of UAP's 1,600 exclusive agents. These stem primarily from the fact that sales agents view the bank branch as an alternative distribution channel constituting a threat to their exclusive distribution privileges and thus their very existence. As a result, unions representing UAP's sales force were antagonistic towards the distribution alliance and sales agents were highly sceptical of the co-operative venture with BNP, doing little to make the sales test a success. In 1990 UAP agents expressed their demands to represent other insurers in addition to UAP in order to compensate for business lost in case UAP increased its use of BNP's branch network as a distribution channel.

In addition, information and training of sales agents concerning BNP's loan products was considered to be insufficient. Finally, sales agents were required to process claims of products sold through the branch network which caused administrative work with no worthwhile pay-off, further increasing motivational problems. These examples underline the difficulties of reconciling two different sales cultures and achieving co-operation of two very different organisational units.

In 1991 BNP decided to change its distribution strategy by establishing 'insurance counters' in the branches of BNP for which UAP takes responsibility. This approach avoids some of the problems which occur when two competing distribution channels owned by two different organisations are supposed to co-operate. In addition, the two firms decided to set up a joint venture in the area of damage insurance. The jointly owned subsidiary, Natio Assurances, will be fully operational in the course of 1993. The new distribution approach appears to be somewhat more successful, as in 1992 45,000 contracts were sold and 1993 sales levels are targeted to reach 55,000. This was less than half the sales level of Crédit Agricole's non-life insurance start-up Pacifica, however.

3.2. Dresdner Bank and Allianz

3.2.1. Background information on the bank and insurer

Dresdner Bank is the second-largest German bank with a capital of ECU 5.8 billion and pre-tax profits ECU 774 million in 1991, 46,000 employees worldwide and almost 1,200 domestic branches serving around 6 million customers.

Allianz which is Europe's largest insurer, had a premium income in 1991 of ECU 22.5 billion and 75,000 employees. It is by far the largest insurer in the German market and was under repeated scrutiny by the domestic competition policy authorities for its dominant position in the domestic insurance market.

3.2.2. Reasons for entering bancassurance and choice of entry vehicle

In April 1989 Dresdner Bank entered a strategic co-operation alliance with Allianz. The main reasons for entering insurance were the increasing share of life insurace products in total savings as well as the perceived potential for diversification and profit enhancement. In contrast to Deutsche Bank which did not hesitate to threaten its client relationship with the large insurers by invading their territory, Dresdner Bank decided "not to upset the relationships with its insurance clients" as noted by a company official in a personal interview. Instead, it opted for exclusive distribution alliances with a few selected insurers, replacing the previous approach of being a broker of a large number of insurers. In eight of the bank's 14 regions Allianz was chosen as the main distributor, while in the other six markets distributors are Victoria and Hamburg-Mannheimer, also owned by Allianz.

In marked contrast to Deutsche Bank, Dresdner Bank has not refrained from striking a number of strategic alliances when entering new markets or expanding its line of business. These include membership in Associated Banks of Europe Corporation (ABECOR), a multilateral co-operation group of a number of European banks and a comprehensive strategic alliance with BNP set up in 1992 including a 10 per cent share swap. Thus, management of Dresdner Bank holds a lot more positive view of the potential benefits and synergy effects of strategic alliances than its main competitor Deutsche Bank.

Due to Allianz' high market share in the German market with almost 25 per cent in life insurance and 17 per cent in non-life business, three times the share of its nearest competitor, the insurer had to undergo repeated scrutiny by the German competition policy authorities. These procedures have made it quite clear that further expansion in the German market through acquisitions would not be tolerated by the Federal Cartel Office. Thus, Allianz looked for a strategic distribution alliance with a bank to find a new distribution channel for its products. It acquired a stake of 5 per cent in Dresdner in 1989 and in 1992 increased its stake to up to 25 per cent. It was forced to reduce this stake to around 23 per cent after rumours spread that it planned to acquire a majority stake in Dresdner which induced the German competition policy authorities to issue a warning statement that it would not tolerate such a financial 'giant'.

Conversely, Dresdner Bank acquired a 10 per cent stake in Allianz.

3.2.3. Marketing and distribution approach to bancassurance

Allianz has a distribution network of more than 5,000 exclusive sales agents and almost 20,000 part-time agents, while Dresdner Bank has around 1,200 branches in Germany. The two companies have a fairly small customer overlap of only about 5 per cent. Thus, the threat of 'cannibalisation' of each other's customer franchise is relatively low. At the same time, this offers significant cross-selling potential for both firms.

Dresdner Bank segments its retail customers according to income and wealth into two clusters which are serviced through different distribution approaches. Accordingly, its marketing strategy for insurance products also differs between the two customer groups. As explained by a bank official in a personal interview, for the lower-income customer group simple products and a high degree of standardisation are desired to achieve fast and cost-efficient distribution, while insurance products for the higher-income group are aimed to be characterised by unique features in order to achieve a degree of product differentiation.

In terms of its distribution approach, the two companies design products which are tailored towards the branch as a distribution channel and can be easily understood and explained by the branch employee. 80 insurance specialists are provided by the insurer to co-ordinate training courses for branch employees. In special circumstances these specialists can be called upon by the branch employee to be present during the consultation with the customer. While most insurance products sold by Dresdner Bank carry the Allianz brand name, Allianz and Dresdner also engage in co-branding products which are distributed through both indigenous channels and where both company names are cited on the product brochures.

Potential customers are identified by branch personnel but this identification process is not supported by database marketing systems.

3.2.4. Incentive structure

Recognising the importance of providing an attractive incentive structure, Dresdner has most recently changed its payment system for insurance products for its branch employees. While bank staff initially received only a small commission which was even completely abolished for a period of time, in September 1992 Dresdner switched to paying its staff a one per cent commission of the total value of the life policy. This new incentive structure is designed as an experiment in order to test the significance of the payment structure. First results indicate that since changing the incentive structure, sales of life policies have picked up considerably.

3.2.5. Success of entry

Results of the distribution alliance have been fairly disappointing until the end of 1992, as a company official concedes in a personal interview. This lack of success was at least partly attributable to an insufficient incentive structure on the part of Dresdner which did not sufficiently motivate its bank employees to cross-sell Allianz products. However, since the incentive structure was changed, sales levels have increased significantly which underlines the importance of payment structures for the success of bancassurance. However, Dresdner Bank has so far not been able to offer the customer a significant advantage by purchasing insurance products through a bank branch rather than from a sales agent. This results from the fact that Allianz products are sold at the same price when sold through a Dresdner Bank branch as when acquired through an Allianz sales agent, a concession which was required in order to avoid upsetting Allianz' vast network of tied agents. The bank hopes to alter this factor by introducing unique products which link banking and insurance features and which will be available only in the bank branches.

3.3. Bank of Scotland and Standard Life

3.3.1. Background information on the bank and insurer

Bank of Scotland is the second-largest regional bank in Scotland behind Royal Bank of Scotland with a branch network of around 400. In 1991 it had a capital size of ECU 1.9 billion and profits of ECU 220 million.

Standard Life is the second-largest life insurer in the UK with a market share in 1989 of 8 per cent and premium volume of

ECU 3.8 billion, following the market leader Prudential which had a 13 per cent market share in that year.

3.3.2. Reasons for entering bancassurance and choice of entry vehicle

Bank of Scotland has distributed both life and non-life insurance products since the 1970s. In the area of life insurance, Bank of Scotland tied to Standard Life in November 1989 which at the same time acquired a 33 per cent stake in the bank. Thus, the strategic distribution alliance is cemented with a significant minority stake of the insurer in the bank which demonstrates commitment of the two co-operating organizations to the area of bancassurance. The main reasons for Bank of Scotland to enter the life insurance market were the perceived profit opportunities in this area and the strategic intent to diversify its income.

Standard Life had a strong interest in expanding its distribution channels, as until recently it only sold through independent financial advisers (IFAs) which was considered to be a too narrow base for expanding business. Thus, it tied with Bank of Scotland and the Halifax, Britain's largest building society, and also introduced financial consultants for those customers which do not have an IFA. As a result, in 1992 the share of IFAs in total sales was reduced from 100 per cent to just under 70 per cent. The alliance with Halifax is phased out by the end of 1994, however, as the building society decided in 1993 to produce life products in-house rather than through means of a distribution alliance.

3.3.3. Marketing and distribution approach

In the area of general insurance, Bank of Scotland distributes household coverage, motor insurance and lending-related creditor insurance under its own brand name. As noted by a company strategist in a personal interview, these three areas were selected as they can be readily linked to the sale of a bank product such as a mortgage, a car loan or a general loan. Thus, "the bank has a clear selling proposition and can even offer package solutions unlike in other areas of general insurance where a bank has no indigenous advantage". All products are underwritten by insurers, however, and claims handling is also processed by the respective insurer.

In the area of life insurance, Bank of Scotland acts as an appointed representative of Standard Life under the provisions of the Financial Services Act. All of the roughly 4,000 retail banking employees of Bank of Scotland have received training devised by Standard Life in order to have a full grasp of its product range. The success of the training was double-checked with an internal examination which had to be passed by all bank employees. Branch staff pass on customers who are potential candidates for life insurance to the so-called financial services consultants which deal exclusively with insurance needs of the customers. In 1993 there were around 110 such consultants which, on average, share between three to four branches. This ratio is aimed to be decreased to one consultant for about two branches. Financial services consultants which were recruited from the bank rather than the insurer were trained by Standard Life and also receive support in terms of product information and labtop computers from the insurer.

3.3.4. Incentive structure

Branch staff does not receive sales commissions and there is no general incentive scheme in place. Since 1980 there exists a profit sharing scheme, however, where employees receive a proportion of between zero and a maximum of six per cent of total allocable profits. The amount depends on the bank's performance measured as the return on equity. Financial services consultants are paid on a salary basis with a bonus payment according to performance. The salary component clearly dominates the bonus, however. As a company official explains in a personal interview, this pay structure was chosen for two reasons. First, consultants were recruited from a banking background and were therefore used to being paid on a salary basis. The transition towards a commission-only pay structure would therefore have "imposed a great strain on the employee". Second, paying employees predominantly on a salary basis is "more compatible with the counselling reputation of a bank, rather than the hard-selling approach usually associated with insurance".

3.3.5. Success of entry

Sales of general insurance products have not increased significantly over the past years. Although no detailed sales figures are disclosed by management, according to a company official the area of general insurance has not experienced tangible growth recently, while in the life insurance sector sales levels have doubled in the past two years. As the company started from a low base, however, this growth rate was below expectations.

3.4. Comparative summary of case studies of distribution alliances

Table 2.6 provides a comparative summary of the three case studies. It becomes apparent that reasons for choosing a distribution alliance differ between individual firms. In addition, the distribution approach also differs with Dresdner selling products through branch staff, while BNP and Bank of Scotland both rely on insurance specialists. None of the cases of entry have so far truly fulfilled initial expectations of management, however.

Table 2.6: Summary table of distribution alliances

	BNP and UAP	Dresdner and Allianz	Bank of Scotland and Standard Life
Background	Third-largest French bank and largest French insurer	Second-largest German bank and Europe's largest insurer	Regional UK bank and second-largest life insurer in the UK
Year and reason for entering alliance	1989; for bank: access to technical skills, for insurer: access to new distribution network	1989; for bank: not upsetting relationships with insurance clients, for insurer: additional growth possible only through new distribution channel	1989; for bank: diversification of income, for insurer: expanding distribution channels
Distribution approach	Changed distribution approach to 'insurance counters' in branches after initial problems	Products primarily sold by branch staff which may call in Allianz consultant	Referrals from branch staff to insurance specialists recruited from bank
Incentive structure	Insurance specialists paid on commission-basis	Recently changed incentive structure to provide commission to branch employee	No incentives for branch employees; insurance specialists primarily salary-based with bonus attached
Success of entry	After initial failure, new distribution approach may contribute to better success	Initial disappointment, but improved sales rates after incentive structure was changed	Growth rates as yet below expectations

4. Joint ventures: sharing risks and profits

A joint venture shall be defined as a legally independent entity which is owned by two or more parent companies which exercise a controlling interest over the venture. In the context of bancassurance, joint ventures are usually between an insurer and a bank which set up a jointly owned firm distributing insurance products to bank customers. Unlike a strategic distribution alliance, it is an organizational form which constitutes a legally separate unit with a management team having clear profit responsibility. In many ways, a joint venture is therefore the limiting case of a strategic alliance, since one could imagine an alliance between two firms establishing a separate organizational unit which comes very close to a joint venture. The difference between a joint venture and a strategic alliance is therefore one of degree and therefore many of the advantages and possible drawbacks are the same for the two entry routes.

The following section discusses three examples of joint ventures in the UK and Germany.

4.1. RBS and Scottish Equitable

4.1.1. Background information on the bank and insurer

Royal Bank of Scotland (RBS) is the sixth-largest UK commercial bank in 1991 with a capital size of ECU 2.5 billion, pre-tax profits of ECU 78 million in 1991, 860 branches in the UK and around 2.75 million customers. In 1992 RBS achieved a profit of ECU 350 million in branch banking which constituted 57 per cent of group profits.

Scottish Equitable which is also based in Edinburgh is a large regional insurer with new annualised premiums of ECU 210 million in 1991.

4.1.2. Reasons for entering bancassurance and choice of entry vehicle

Similarly to BNP, Royal Bank has followed a mix of entry routes into the insurance sector. It entered non-life insurance through de novo entry, while entering life insurance through means of a joint venture which is exactly the reverse of BNP.

In 1985 RBS set up a subsidiary, Direct Line, which distributes motor insurance through means of direct marketing, as it perceived a market niche for a low-cost insurer which relies on the telephone as the main delivery channel. This distribution channel is convenient for the customer and at the same time highly cost-effective for the supplier.[8] Direct Line's distribution process is based on telephone sales where customers call in, give information about risk-determining factors such as age, occupation and claims history and immediately get a quote of the relevant premium which is calculated by an expert system fed by a large database of previous claims. Due to the fact that Direct Line does not employ any sales offices and pays no commission to agents it is able to offer significantly lower premiums than the large established insurers. Due to this price advantage and an aggressive advertising campaign, Direct Line has been the fastest-growing insurance business in the UK and is the only UK insurer which consistently achieves an underwriting profit. It has the lowest cost/premiums ratio in the motor insurance sector and by 1992 has achieved a leading position in the motor insurance sector with 670,000 policies in force. Total profits for Direct Line were ECU 20 million in 1992, a 50 per cent increase compared to 1991. It is planned to further broaden Direct Line's product portfolio by adding a range of financial products. It is important to note that Direct Line does not directly cross-sell to the retail customers of RBS. This is due to the fact that management considers an insurance relationship to be different from a banking relationship and does not want to jeopardise the link between bank and customer if there are disputes concerning insurance claims. Thus, the corporate image of Direct Line is kept quite distinct from that of the Royal Bank.

Despite the success with direct marketing general insurance products, RBS established a joint venture in 1990 for the life sector with Scottish Equitable (SE) in order to access the accumulated know-how of the insurer. SE was chosen due to its product focus and substantial experience in the area of unit-linked and savings products.

SE took a 5 per cent stake in RBS. This stake was at least partly designed to reduce the chance of a hostile takeover of RBS through spreading equity stakes to 'friendly' stakeholders.

The newly-founded joint venture, Royal Scottish Assurance, also had the strategic objective of securing insurance profits for RBS which aimed at gaining a share of the large pool of life insurance premiums. On the part of SE, management perceived an opportunity to diversify its distribution channels by expanding into the bank's retail network.

Both partners initially invested ECU 26 million in the venture. Initially, RBS owned 51 per cent and SE 49 per cent of Royal Scottish Assurance, but later RBS increased its stake to 75 per cent, with the option of increasing it up to 80 per cent. Top management of the joint venture is dominated by insurance executives, however, with 3 out of 4 directors (including the CEO) being former general managers of SE and one director coming from RBS.

4.1.3. Marketing and distribution approach to bancassurance

Royal Scottish which started business in October 1990 has a capital of ECU 26 million and employs around 240 insurance sales agents in mid-1993. It is planned to increase this number to 300 by 1994. It sells life and pension products, unit trusts and Personal Equity Plans to the bank's retail customers as well as offering financial health 'check-ups' employing labtop computers.

The distribution concept aims at establishing close co-operation between agents and branch personnel. It is part of the sales agents' task to train branch employees in insurance matters and almost 4,000 branch staff have so far been trained. Actual distribution is shared by branch staff and insurance agents, where branch employees are responsible for selling simple life products such as term insurance and mortgage-related endowments. For more complicated products which require a higher level of know-how, customers are referred to insurance specialists of Royal Scottish who are responsible for one to four branches, similar to TSB sales agents. There is therefore a mixture of distribution channels with retail branch employees being the first point of sales for the customer.

In terms of pricing, some products are sold at better conditions than those of SE, while others are sold at a higher price. As a company official explains in a personal interview, this stems from a different product mix of Royal Scottish compared to SE which necessitates a different pricing structure.

The bank segments its customer base according to areas of residence through the post code as well as in terms of income through means of transaction analysis. This allows specific targeting of customers who are likely candidates for acquiring life insurance or investment products.

Organisationally, Royal Scottish, which is legally separated from the two mother companies, is being charged by SE for administrative tasks such as premium handling and claims processing, for assessment and management of actuarial risk and for investment services. It benefits from joint product development with SE. RBS supplies branch space and employees at no service charge, but receives 50 per cent of the commission of any policy sold by Royal Scottish.

4.1.4. Incentive structure

Financial compensation of insurance specialists is primarily on a salary basis with a small bonus attached which is rewarded according to performance.

Close co-operation with branch personnel is encouraged by making the branch the smallest organisational unit of awarding a bonus rather than individual agents. Thus, insurance agents and branch personnel maximise a joint utility function rather than working towards different goals. Branches are rewarded a commission for every lead passed on to an insurance specialist which leads to a sale. However, this commission is only about one third the level of that usually paid to an IFA and thus distrubution costs are significantly lower.

Insurance specialists are paid between ECU 21,000 and ECU 29,000. In addition, they receive a small bonus which is rewarded according to performance. As a company official notes in a personal interview, this payment structure "takes away the need for the insurance specialist to place pressure on the customer and engage in aggressive selling tactics. It accords better with the image of the bank as a counsellor in financial services acting in the customer's best interest".

4.1.5. Success of entry

After the first six months of operation, Royal Scottish achieved a daily sales rate of around 100 policies. 14,000 policies were sold in the first year of operation and annualised premiums reached

ECU 11 million. In 1992 annualised premiums increased to ECU 25 million. By the end of 1992, 50,000 policies had been sold. Profits were ECU 0.4 million in 1991 and ECU 2.6 million in 1992, while ECU 6 million were paid in commission to branches. Expected profits in 1993 are ECU 8 million.

Since the current penetration rate of RBS's customer base is only around three per cent, management perceives significant growth potential. The customer base which is expected to reach 100,000 by early 1994 is predicted to grow to around 450,000 by the end of 1996 according to internal company projections.

4.2. Commerzbank and DBV

4.2.1. Background information on the bank and insurer

Commerzbank is the third-largest German bank with a branch network of almost 1,000, 3.5 million retail customers, capital of ECU 7.3 billion and pre-tax profits of ECU 950 million in 1991.

Deutsche Beamtenversicherung (DBV) had premiums of ECU 1.5 billion in 1992 and is active in all lines of life and general insurance including health and legal protection. It has a special focus on government employees and in 1989 had an overall market share of 2 per cent in the German life insurance sector. DBV Holding is one of the ten largest quoted insurers in Germany. Profits in 1992 were ECU 21 million, compared to ECU 8 million in the previous year. It has a customer franchise of more than 2 million policyholders.

4.2.2. Reasons for entering bancassurance and choice of entry vehicle

In 1989 DBV altered its group structure to become a publicly quoted company with a holding company replacing the former public ownership structure and floating 49.9 per cent of its shares. 25 per cent of this holding company were held by the public authorities, another 25 per cent plus one share was acquired by Commerzbank, while 49.9 per cent were widely spread across 30,000 shareholders. In 1992 Commerzbank increased its stake to 48.2 per cent. Thus, Commerzbank and the publicly owned holding company together hold a majority stake in DBV Holding which can therefore be considered a joint venture.

As a bank official notes in a personal interview, Commerzbank decided to acquire a stake in DBV, as it perceived a need to expand into insurance after its main competitors, Deutsche and Dresdner Bank, had already entered this sector. In addition, it observed that in order to be able to fully satisfy the financial needs of its customers, life insurance products increasingly became indispensable in the bank's product portfolio. As the bank official notes, this stems from the fact that "in the customer's perception banking and insurance products are increasingly seen as complementary services". The joint venture route with DBV was chosen in order to quickly acquire the necessary product and distribution know-how to establish a rapid presence in the field of insurance.

On the part of DBV, the insurer perceived an attractive opportunity to broaden its distribution channels and gain access to Commerzbank's retail branch network.

4.2.3. Marketing and distribution approach to bancassurance

Starting in May 1990, Commerzbank and DBV opened their respective distribution channels to the products of the partner. Thus, Commerzbank distributes DBV products through its 1,000 branches, while DBV's sales network of around 18,400 part-time and around 2,000 full-time employees distributes Commerzbank's loan and mortgage products. DBV has changed its company logo to include the sentence that it is "partner of Commerzbank". The strategic relation between the two firms is thus made explicit to the general public. In addition, DBV undertook an extensive advertising campaign which highlighted the new alliance between Commerzbank and DBV.

The distribution approach differs between life and non-life products. While life insurance is distributed directly by bank staff, bank customers who are interested in non-life products are referred to DBV sales agents who are assigned to the particular branch. As a bank official notes in a personal interview, the distribution approach for life insurance has been significantly more successful than for non-life insurance, despite the fact that bank staff does not receive any commission. This stems primarily from the fact that "life products are much closer in spirit to traditional bank products", while bank staff has greater difficulties recognising selling opportunities for general insurance. In addition, general insurance has lower commission levels and therefore the incentive for DBV staff to actively sell these products to bank customers is lower.

Similarly to Dresdner Bank, Commerzbank has stratified its customer base according to income into two clusters which are served by different customer advisers. In the area of insurance, however, there is no differentiation in terms of products between the two groups.

4.2.4. Incentive structure

The bank does not offer any kind of incentives to its employees. While such incentive schemes have been contemplated and are considered to be desirable by management, there has so far been stiff resistance by the company worker council (*Betriebsrat*) which opposes any move towards pay for performance systems.

4.2.5. Success of entry

The distribution agreement has so far been more successful for branches selling insurance products than agents selling bank products. After including insurance in its product portfolio in May 1990 Commerzbank sold whole life insurance with a total value of up to ECU 500 million per annum. In the year from May 1990 to April 1991 Commerzbank sold a share of 16 per cent of DBV's new business through its branch network. Distribution of bank products through DBV's sales network, however, started off a lot slower and was "particularly difficult in its initial phase", as noted by the Commerzbank Director responsible for the alliance (Korff and Dorner, 1991, p. 19). As a Commerzbank official explains in a personal interview, the reason for the slow sales of bank products is simply that commissions for selling these products are low compared to those of insurance products. Thus, in the priority list of sales agents, bank products are certainly not at the top. Nevertheless, sales of bank products through the sales agent network increased from ECU 100 million in 1991 to ECU 190 million in 1992 with mortgage products predominating.

4.3. Midland Bank and Commercial Union

4.3.1. Background information on the bank and insurer

Midland Bank is the fourth-largest UK bank with a total capital of ECU 3.8 billion, pre-tax profits of ECU 60 million in 1991 and 1,740 branches. In 1992 it was acquired by the Hongkong and Shanghai Banking group which has a capital of ECU 5.7 billion and pre-tax profits of ECU 1.4 billion in 1991.

Commercial Union is one of the largest UK insurers with a market share of around 2.8 per cent in the life sector with premiums of ECU 1,350 million in 1989 and a market share of 9.4 per cent in the non-life sector with premiums of ECU 3,300 million in 1989.

4.3.2. Reasons for entering bancassurance and choice of entry vehicle

In 1987 the two firms decided to set up a joint venture company called Midland Life (ML) which started operations in April 1988. ML was initially owned 60 per cent by Midland and 40 per cent by CU. Later Midland increased its stake, however, and currently CU holds only 12 per cent of ML's capital. It is the intention of the management of both CU and Midland to reduce this stake further. Thus, what initially started as a joint venture has now essentially become a wholly-owned subsidiary of Midland.

As is explained by a Midland official in a personal interview, the joint venture route was initially chosen to gain a rapid entry into the insurance sector, since Midland's know-how base was negligible when the decision to actively enter insurance was taken in 1987. Thus, management perceived that through entering a joint venture with a large and experienced insurance company a know-how base could be rapidly built up which would allow successful entry. As noted by the company official: "the decision to enter into an alliance with the Commercial Union was predominantly motivated by the perceived necessity to gain a speedy entry. In contrast to our competitors, Midland had only marginal insurance business in 1987 and the significant existing business potential was to be tapped rapidly". In addition, CU was identified as one of the few insurance firms which was willing to take a minority stake in the firm and had no intentions of exercising a controlling interest in the joint venture.

4.3.3. Marketing and distribution approach to bancassurance

Administrative and information technology services were initially undertaken by CU against a fee, while Midland Bank received a commission for any policy sold through its branch network, an agreement similar to that of RBS and SE. During the first phase of operation Midland Life recruited a sales force from its own ranks, but later recruited employees from outside the bank. Its life insurance sales force at the end of 1992 consisted of around 500 agents, with a further increase to 700 planned by the end of 1993.

Initially, Midland aimed at a branch-based distribution concept where life insurance sales were made by regular branch employees. For this purpose, Midland trained up to 8,000 branch staff in the selling of life insurance. Success of this training scheme did not live up to expectations, however, since sales results by branch employees were less than anticipated. According to a company official, it turned out that there were 'cultural' problems with selling life insurance and since there was no clear incentive structure in place to motivate branch staff to actively engage in selling, there were motivational problems on the part of branch employees.

As a result, Midland Life decided to introduce a distribution concept similar to that of TSB with insurance consultants being based in branches. There are two ways for customers to be referred to the life insurance specialist. Firstly, customers who express an interest in life insurance are offered an appointment with an insurance specialist. Interest by customers is stimulated through product-specific direct marketing campaigns which are undertaken throughout the whole year and which target customers who are most likely to have an interest in a particular product. Secondly, potential customers for life insurance are identified by the branch manager or senior branch personnel according to specific criteria such as lack of sound retirement provisions, for example, and to these customers branch personnel proactively suggests to make an appointment with the insurance consultant. The senior branch employee who is the account manager for the particular customer introduces the customer to the insurance agent and may even stay with the customer throughout the first consultation.

ML offers the full product range of life insurance, rather than focusing on a subset of products. Its strategic objective is to function as an allround financial services supplier which can provide the whole range of financial products.

Its organisational structure at the level of headquarters is similar to that of Barclays. In 1991 all insurance activities, unit trust business, retail stockbroking and investment services for high net-worth individuals were brought together to form Midland Financial Services.

4.3.4. Incentive structure

Midland does not provide its branch employees with financial incentives to pass on customers to insurance consultants. Instead, branch managers attempt to create and foster a 'team spirit' among branch personnel and insurance agents where the customer is the focus of attention. However, no formal group incentive scheme is in place which would help to support this team-building effort. Branch managers are responsible for the profitability of their entire customer franchise and this includes insurance products. Thus, branch managers have an incentive to maximise insurance sales as well as other banking products. To reduce potential 'cultural' problems between salaried branch employees and insurance specialists who receive a commission on top of their base salary, Midland has provided for a career route for branch employees who feel that their strength lies in selling life insurance. These branch employees can train to become insurance consultants. Thus, the cultural divide between insurance agents and branch employees is reduced, since the career path of an insurance consultant is principally open to every branch employee.

4.3.5. Success of entry

In 1990 new single premiums were ECU 180 million and new regular premiums were ECU 16 million. By 1991 around 120,000 policies had been sold. In 1992 life insurance income increased by 30 per cent with total operating income of Midland Financial Services standing at ECU 270 million. While ML does not reveal separate profit figures, ML officials stress that profitability has been very satisfactory. However, Midland Life has been less successful in penetrating its banking customer base where it is estimated that it has reached a share of only about 3 per cent of its retail customers. Thus, compared to the 30 per cent penetration rate of Bank of Ireland's Lifetime, for example, ML clearly has some catching up to do.

4.4. Comparative summary of case studies of joint ventures

Table 2.7 provides a summary of the joint ventures. It becomes apparent that distribution approaches differ just like for the case studies of distribution alliances. While RBS and Commerzbank both employ branch staff for distribution, Midland relies on specialists, similar to the TSB approach. The examined joint ventures have so far been relatively more successful than distribution alliances, but less successful than de novo entries.

Table 2.7: Summary table of joint ventures

	RBS and Scottish Equitable	Commerzbank and DBV	Midland and Commercial Union
Background	Sixth-largest UK bank and large regional insurer	Third-largest German bank and one of ten largest German insurers	Fourth-largest UK bank and tenth-largest UK life insurer
Year and reason for entering JV	1990; for bank: sharing into life insurance profits, for insurer: diversification of distribution channels	1989; for bank: to catch up with competition which had already entered insurance, for insurer: to broaden distribution channels	1987; for bank: to catch up with competitors, for insurer: portfolio investment
Distribution approach	Simple products sold by branch staff, more complicated products by SE specialists	Life insurance sold directly by branch staff, non-life by DBV agent	Referrals from branch staff to insurance specialists recruited from bank
Incentive structure	Specialists paid on salary basis with small bonus attached, branches rewarded commissions for passing on successful leads	No incentives for branch staff	No formal incentive scheme in place
Success of entry	Appears relatively successful, but too early to assess	More successful in life than in non-life insurance	Satisfactory growth rates but customer penetration currently only 3 per cent

5. Mergers and acquisitions: integrating banking and insurance organizations

5.1. Merger or majority acquisition

A majority acquisition of an insurance firm or a merger between a bank and insurer have the advantage that it is possible to draw on insurance know-how and an established sales organization. This form of entry is frequently chosen because it entails significant expertise and experience in the insurance sector.

The next section analyses three case studies of mergers and acquisitions in the UK and the Netherlands.

5.2. NMB Postbank and Nationale Nederlanden

5.2.1. Background information on the bank and insurer

NMB Postbank was the third-largest Dutch bank with a capital of ECU 3.0 billion in 1990 and resulted from the 1989 merger between the two formerly independent groups, Nederlandsche Mittenstandsbank (NMB) which has more than 400 branches and the formerly state-owned Postbank which uses more than 2,100 post offices and agencies as retail outlets. It has market shares of 41 per cent in payment accounts and 22 per cent in the savings and deposit market.

Nationale Nederlanden was the largest insurer in the Netherlands and the sixth-largest insurer in Europe with a premium volume of ECU 7 billion in 1989. It has a distribution network of more than 10,000 independent and 1,200 tied insurance intermediaries. In 1991 its market share in life insurance is 24 per cent and 10 per cent in non-life insurance.

In 1992 ING group attained profits before taxation of ECU 480 million in its banking operations and ECU 520 million in its insurance business.

5.2.2. Reasons for entering bancassurance and choice of entry vehicle

In March 1991 the two groups completed a merger to form Internationale Nederlanden Group (ING). Such cross-shareholdings between banks and insurers were legalised in the Netherlands only at the beginning of 1990 and resulted in a number of cross-industry participations such as Rabobank which acquired insurer Interpolis in 1990 and the merger between AMEV and Verenigde Spaarbanken in the same year.

The strategic rationale for the merger was partly defensive to prevent a hostile takeover, but also to reap benefits of economies of scale and scope and to secure a position in the Dutch market increasingly characterised by a high degree of concentration in financial services. It is estimated that the three largest banks have a market share of more than 90 per cent when measured in terms of total assets. Virtually all financial institutions have entered the insurance sector. In addition, as a company official notes, diversification was another motivator to enter the insurance market, as insurance is expected to contribute to a more stable flow of income.

A merger was chosen rather than a joint venture or a distribution alliance because "a merger means one vision throughout the company, one policy, one strategy and one responsibility in one board", as noted by a company official. A joint venture, in contrast, was perceived to provide commitment problems on the part of the joint venture partners and in the words of an official it was repudiated becuase "the lifecycle of joint ventures has shown that after a few years cracks emerge in such a relationship".

After the merger, the ING group has become the largest financial institution in the Netherlands with total assets in 1992 of ECU 145 billion, a group capital of almost ECU 7.7 billion and 51,000 employees.

5.2.3. *Marketing and distribution approach to bancassurance*

Before the merger, Nationale Nederlanden employed independent brokers as their main distribution channel for both life and non-life products, accounting for 80 per cent of total product sales of Nat-Ned. Brokers represent by far the most important distribution channel in the Dutch market accounting for 60 per cent of overall distribution. Brokers, of course, fear the increase in competition which results when an insurer adds the bank branch as a new distribution channel. This results from the fact that insurance products sold through bank branches can be offered at significantly better conditions than those sold through agents and brokers, since distribution costs are lower. Thus, brokers fear that when competing with bank branches they are likely to lose a significant share of their sales to this less costly distribution channel, in particular when the insurer is willing to offer the same or similar products at a lower price when bought through the bank channel.

In order to preserve their delicate balance with the network of brokers and independent financial intermediaries, both AMEV and Interpolis were careful in their communication with brokers. In particular, they emphasised that they had no intention of offering identical or similar products at a lower price when sold through a bank branch. ING, however, made no such assurances and even announced plans to offer specially designed products which were to be offered through its branch network. Brokers therefore decided in November 1990 to boycott ING's products until a clear statement to withdraw such plans was made by the company management. ING which came into existence after the merger transaction was completed in March 1991 was soon forced to submit to the pressure exercised by brokers. In September 1991 the boycott officially ended after ING assured brokers that it was going to use the NMB-Postbank branch network to sell only simple insurance products which pose no significant threat to the brokers' share of total insurance sales.

The organisational structure of the ING group up to 1993 did not provide for major integration between insurance and banking units. In order to change this lack of integration, management decided to create a new organizational structure to be implemented in late 1993 and 1994. This new structure consists of four major profit centres which are domestic business, international business, real estate and investment management.

So far, co-operation between Nat-Ned and NMB-Postbank has started in the area of distribution where Nat-Ned's agents have begun to sell banking products including savings and deposits accounts with loan facilities developed by Nat-Ned Financial Services. Postbank, on the other hand, started to enter insurance business by founding two subsidiaries in life and general business which underwrite and distribute their own products through the Postbank's retail network and through direct marketing activities. In May 1991 Postbank started selling single-premium policies and for the rest of that year achieved sales of ECU 60 million. Two general insurance products were introduced in the second half of 1991. In addition, a simple life policy was designed to be distributed via ING Bank branches. In order to distribute this product, 3,500 branch employees were trained as they constitute the first point of contact. The actual sale is carried out by the Nat-Ned agent, however.

5.2.4. Success of entry

The merger between Nat-Ned and NMB-Postbank was viewed with significant scepticism by shareholders of Nationale Nederlanden Group who regarded their stocks as undervalued. In addition to these quarrels with shareholders during the merger negotiations and problems encountered with Nat-Ned's broker network, there were integration difficulties in the post-merger process of NMB and Postbank. The fact that branches needed to change names twice in only three years - from NMB to NMB-Postbank and subsequently to ING Bank - did not help to sustain a persistent corporate image with customers.

The potential for synergy effects in the international network is limited, since the insurance subsidiaries are mainly active in the retail field, whereas the international banking units operate almost exclusively in the corporate sector.

By giving in to the brokers' demands, the merger between NMB-Postbank and Nat-Ned may have lost its most significant strategic rationale. This stems from the fact that pooling the two customer franchises is no longer possible and the bank branch channel which is the most powerful tool in bancassurance distribution cannot be utilised up to its full potential. While it is too early for a comprehensive assessment of the merger, it does not seem unlikely that ING will change its defensive stance towards brokers, once it believes that it has established its branch network in a way which can substitute the brokers' network. While there would be an inevitable slump in sales in the short run, the customer base of NMB-Postbank could constitute a powerful replacement in the longer run. ING's 1992 annual report noted that insurance sales through bank branches have increased significantly which seems to confirm the notion that this channel will be increasingly used to distribute insurance products despite the brokers' protests. According to a company official, the overall synergy effect of the merger stemming from additional revenues as well as cost savings is estimated to be around ECU 27 million.

Overall, it is too early to assess the success of the merger between the two firms. However, it is clear that the merger process has certainly not been a smooth ride and that many of the initial expectations concerning synergy potentials have so far at least been disappointed. As the company chairman of ING Group concedes:

> when one merges companies there are conflicts of interests between people and organisations as well as different systems [such as] administrative systems or social systems ... [which] never really make things easier ... People are experts in generating reasons why things are not possible in the ING Group. So you have to put a lot of energy in mobilising the workforce (Jacobs, 1993).

5.3. Lloyds and Abbey Life

5.3.1. Background information on the bank and insurer

Lloyds Bank is the third-largest UK bank with a capital of ECU 4.3 billion in 1991, a branch network of almost 2,000 and a customer franchise of 6 million. In 1992 it achieved profits before tax of ECU 1,050 million and was thus the most profitable UK retail bank.

Abbey Life had a market share of 2.3 per cent in 1989 and a premium volume of ECU 1,100 million. In the unit-linked market it has the second-highest market share and has a reputation of being a product innovator in that area. It has a sales force of 3,200 self-employed agents and almost 700 sales offices.

5.3.2. Reasons for entering insurance and choice of entry vehicle

In December 1988 Abbey Life merged with 5 of Lloyds insurance business subsidiaries which were Black Horse Life and Lloyds Bank Unit Trust Companies to form Black Horse Financial Services (BJFS), Lloyds Bank Insurance Services (LBIS), an insurance broker, Black Horse Agencies, a chain of real estates and Lloyds Bowmaker, a finance company. In return, Lloyds acquired a 58 per cent stake in Abbey Life.

The strategic rationale for the acquisition was to acquire the know-how base of Abbey Life to improve the life insurance business which it started early 1988 and to offer one-stop shopping to customers. In addition, there was perceived to be a need for diversification into a low-risk, high-margin sector such as life insurance and to generate more fee-based income from its retail branch network. Insurance business was considered to provide a stable stream of income which is less prone to business fluctuations than many retail banking activities. The main strategic rationale to enter a merger was to cement a strategic relationship with the insurer. While a joint venture was also considered, management felt that a merger would provide more stability and a clearer signal to both employees and the market that Lloyds Bank was serious about the concept of bancassurance. De novo entry was excluded due to the fact that management felt that the required know-how base and expertise required to establish a successful life insurance business in a short period of time could not be built up sufficiently quickly. This know-how base concerned not only the actual production and underwriting of life insurance contracts but in particular sales and marketing expertise.

Abbey Life welcomed the friendly acquisition, since it perceived an opportunity to broaden its customer base and add a new distribution channel with Lloyds' extensive branch network. Strategically, it aimed at improving productivity which it perceived to be too low with about one sale per week and sales agent, compared to TSB's 4 to 5 sales per week.

The new organisational unit was named Lloyds Abbey Life and comprises Abbey Life, Black Horse Financial Services, Lloyds Bank Insurance Services, the European subsidiaries, Lloyds Bowmaker Finance and Black Horse Agencies.

5.3.3. Marketing and distribution approach to bancassurance

Soon after the merger sales and marketing executives of Abbey Life joined the management team of Black Horse Financial Services (BHFS). More than 3,000 Lloyds branch employees were trained in the first year alone in the sale of life insurance products. BHFS's distribution approach is similar but not identical to that of TSB. In 1992 about 1,000 sales consultants and 900 dedicated bank employees specialise in selling life insurance. Thus, in contrast to TSB which only employs sales agents, but similarly to Royal Bank of Scotland, Lloyds Bank also trains a selection of its own branch employees to sell life insurance products directly. Bank employees mostly focus on transaction-related life products such as mortgage endowment, bonds and other savings products. Where the bank employee feels that a more comprehensive financial analysis is required, she passes the customer along to the insurance agent. Insurance agents perform full-fledged financial analyses for customers and offer these services not only in the branches but visit customers outside branch opening hours. In addition, the sales force is primarily responsible for those Lloyds customers who do not visit their branches regularly. A Lloyds Abbey Life official explains in a personal interview that "we aim to fully penetrate our customer base by following up not only the warm leads but also by exploring other indications of buying disposition such as certain customer characteristics. It is these colder leads which are followed up by the sales force".

In 1991 insurance consultants were actually integrated into the branches for a number of reasons. Firstly, test results in a number of trial branches showed that when insurance consultants are based in branches, co-operation between branch employees and consultants improves significantly. In addition, the UK Banking Code of Practice requires that leads about customers can only be passed on to other bank employees. Thus, insurance agents need to be legally employed by the bank. Finally, cultural problems between bank employees and insurance agents could be reduced by day-to-day contact and improving mutual communication. A company official notes that initial hostilities "which inadvertently result when combing two very different sales and corporate cultures" have been reduced by this co-operative approach.

5.3.4. Incentive structure

There is a certain degree of internal competition between bank staff and sales agents who have a functional overlap when selling life insurance products. Bank employees are compensated on a regular salary basis with no attached bonus or commissions for selling insurance products. Sales agents are also compensated on a salary basis but de facto face a pay for performance structure, as they have to reach a certain commission level to receive their salary. Thus, every sales agent is given certain target levels for selling life insurance products.

Similarly, branches are given target levels for selling insurance products. Senior branch personnel and regional directors are rewarded at least partly according to meeting these targets. In addition, branches receive a commission for each warm lead which is passed on to an insurance consultant by branch staff. In 1992, 51 per cent of annualised sales were made through Lloyd's branch network, a slight decrease compared to the previous year. Sales via Black Horse consultants increased, however, by 71 per cent and now account for 38 per cent of annualised sales.

As a company official concedes, an apparent problem with this kind of incentive structure is that it is crucially dependent on the success of sales management by branch managers. This stems from the fact that unlike the branch manager, bank employees have no direct financial incentive to deal with the customer who wants to acquire life insurance but may as well pass her on to the sales force. Thus, the branch manager needs to motivate her staff accordingly to ensure that the target levels of insurance sales are reached. Motivational stimulus is provided, for example, by the prospect of being promoted sooner if sales performance surpasses certain levels. A Lloyds Abbey Life official notes that while more performance-oriented pay also for branch staff would be desirable, it has so far not been introduced due to perceived practical and conceptual problems.

5.3.5. Success of entry

BHFS has experienced significant growth since inception. Regular premium sales in 1992 reached ECU 87 million, while single premium sales amounted to ECU 940 million, an increase of 92 per cent compared to 1990.

Figure 2.3 provides a comparison of growth rates of new annualised premiums for Abbey Life and BHFS. It becomes obvious that Black Horse has experienced dramatic growth with a compound annual growth rate of 24 per cent between 1988 and 1992, while Abbey Life has experienced virtually no growth in the past four years. While Black Horse Financial Services experienced rapid growth since its inception with the number of salespeople increasing from 100 in 1988 to more than 700 in 1992, Abbey Life's performance largely stagnated. In 1992 new annualised premiums of BHFS even surpassed those of Abbey Life for the first time.

Part of the reason why Abbey Life's performance has not profited from the merger is that its organisational structure was largely unaffected by the acquisition. Its sales agent network does not have access to the bank's customer base and sells life insurance in the 'traditional' way through cold calling and home visits rather than warm calls and using branches as the main distribution channel like Black Horse. It has an indigenous customer franchise of around 1 million policyholders. Half of new sales are made to the existing customer clientele. The sales cultures of the two competing units are quite different as well. While Abbey Life's sales agents are referred to as "hunters", Black Horse sales agents are called "farmers".

Figure 2.3: New annualised premiums of Black Horse Financial Services and Abbey Life from 1988 to 1992

£ millions

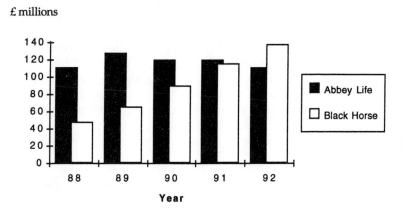

Note: Annualised premiums are calculated as new regular premiums plus one-tenth of single premiums

Source: Annual reports and direct contacts with Lloyds Abbey Life.

Table 2.8 analyses profits of Lloyds Abbey Life between 1988 and 1992. It becomes apparent that Black Horse Financial Services has experienced significantly greater profit growth with a compound annual growth rate of 23 per cent than Abbey Life which only had a CAGR of 3 per cent between 1988 and 1992.

In 1992 Lloyds Abbey Life's profits constituted 37 per cent of Lloyds Bank's total profits and was by far the most profitable business unit of the group which underlines the significant contribution which insurance services make towards total group profits of Lloyds Bank.

Lloyds Abbey Life's management still sees significant growth potential for cross-selling insurance products to the 6 million Lloyds Bank customers. It notes that of all Lloyds bank customers purchasing insurance at any time, 84 per cent have yet to purchase their insurance through Lloyds Abbey Life. Of the 1.2 million Lloyds Bank customers with life insurance policies only 16 per cent have purchased their policy through Lloyds Abbey Life up to the year 1992. While this percentage constitutes a significant increase from the 1988 level when only 2 per cent of Lloyds customers acquired their insurance through a branch, management of Lloyds Abbey Life expects to be able to raise this stake even further to 35 per cent by 1995.

Table 2.8: Analysis of profits after tax of Lloyds Abbey Life between 1988 and 1992

in ECU million

	Abbey Life Assurance	BHFS
1988	113	36
1989	121	38
1990	121	60
1991	137	84
1992	132	100
CAGR	+3.1%	+23.3%

CAGR: Compound Annual Growth Rate
Source: Annual Reports.

When assessing the merger between the two firms, economic benefits seem limited due to lack of integration between Abbey Life and Black Horse. While some of this lack of integration is explained by regulatory constraints, the overall result has not lived up to expectations of the pre-merger phase. A company official confirms that "synergy effects between Abbey Life and Black Horse have turned out to be less than initially expected".

According to this company official, the most significant side effect of the merger may so far have been the infusion of a sales-oriented approach into the transaction and processing-oriented culture of the bank.

5.4. Rabobank and Interpolis

5.4.1. Background information on the bank and insurer

The Rabobank Group is a Dutch co-operative bank with a capital in 1991 of ECU 6.7 billion and pre-tax profits of ECU 780 million and has a similar ownership structure as French Crédit Agricole. It is owned by around 790 local banks and has the largest domestic retail branch network with 2,100 branches and around 1,000 agencies in the Netherlands. It accounts for 90 per cent of all bank credit granted to the agricultural sector in the Netherlands. It has a 40 per cent market share in retail business with an estimated 9 million savings accounts. In addition, 30 per cent of the domestic mortgage market are handled by Rabobank and it accounts for a third of all payment transactions.

Interpolis is the fifth-largest insurer in the Netherlands with a 6 per cent market share in both general and life insurance. It also has a co-operative ownership structure, similar to that of Rabobank.

5.4.2. Reasons for entering insurance and choice of entry vehicle

Rabobank has had a long-standing strategic distribution alliance with Interpolis. Rabobank thus became the largest single distributor of Interpolis' products accounting for a share of around three quarters in 1989. Before public regulations restricting cross-industry ownership between banking and insurance were relaxed in 1990, Rabobank owned 15 per cent of Interpolis which was the maximum allowed under the old regulatory regime.

In May 1990 Rabobank decided to increase its stake in Interpolis from 10 per cent to 95 per cent and subsequently to 100 per cent. As a company official notes in a personal interview, this decision was primarily motivated by the fact that large amounts of savings funds were withdrawn from regular bank savings products and placed into tax-advantaged life insurance policies.

As noted by the company official, Interpolis was the most obvious choice for an acquisition for Rabobank among insurance companies, since the two firms not only had a long-established distribution alliance but also share a similar corporate culture due to their co-operative ownership structure and their focus on the agricultural sector.

5.4.3. Marketing and distribution approach and incentive structure

Every Rabobank branch has an insurance desk staffed by branch employees with specialist know-how in insurance. Sales commissions are paid to branches rather than individual employees. Training of branch employees is provided by Interpolis which is also responsible for product development.

Rabobank has become the predominant distribution channel for Interpolis, as it accounts for more than 90 per cent of new sales, up from 75 per cent before the merger. It has sold insurance polices to about one third of Rabobank customers.

As a company official notes, "insurance is traditionally a product that has to be brought to the customer. It is therefore imperative to have a clear concept concerning segmentation of the market". In order to facilitate identification of potential customers Rabobank and Interpolis have therefore stratified their customer base. It is divided according to six criteria which include simple or complex product requirements, active and passive attitude of the customer describing the approach to the purchase of insurance, and the customer's preferred distribution channel, in particular distinguishing between direct distribution versus an advice-based distribution channel such as the branch or an insurance intermediary. The application of these criteria leads to seven segments. For example, the segment "Simple Requirements of Active People via the Advice Channel" describes a segment characterised by

> young people with a good education who have just started working ... and need good advice to help them get all the possibilities into perspective ... they want to get to know a certain amount about the products and are willing to switch suppliers if expectations are better met by a different supplier.

In a similar fashion, Rabobank has defined the other segments and attempts to create distinctive products and tailored distribution channels for the different groups.

5.4.4. Success of entry

Growth rates of life gross premium income after the merger in 1990 turned out to be disappointing. Gross premiums in life insurance were ECU 690 million, an increase of only 2 per cent compared to the pre-merger premium level, well below the industry growth rate. In 1991 Interpolis only managed to maintain its gross premium level compared to an industry growth rate of more than 10 per cent and therefore lost relative market share. In non-life insurance Interpolis was relatively more sucessful, increasing its market share with gross premiums in non-life insurance of ECU 585 million in 1992. Net profits of Interpolis in 1992 were ECU 29 million, a decrease compared to net profits of ECU 53 million in the pre-merger year 1989. In summary, Rabobank's merger with Interpolis has so far not fulfilled management's expectations concerning exploitation of synergy effects.

5.5. Comparative summary of case studies of mergers and acquisitions

Table 2.9 provides a summary of the three case studies of mergers and acquisitions.

Table 2.9: Summary table of mergers and acquisitions

	NMB Postbank and NatNed	Lloyds and Abbey Life	Rabobank and Interpolis
Background	Third-largest Dutch bank and largest Dutch insurer	Third-largest UK bank and fifteenth-largest life insurer	Second-largest Dutch bank and fifth-largest insurer, both co-operatively owned
Year and reason for merger or acquisition	1991: merger; to reap benefits of economies of scale and scope	1985: acquisition; for bank: diversification and know-how synergy effects, for insurer: adding new distribution channel	1990: acquisition; for bank: to increase share in life insurance market and reap benefits from synery;
Distribution approach	Mutual cross-selling has started	Branch staff as well as insurance consultants based in branches	Specialist branch staff on insurance desk
Incentive structure	No information available	No commission for branch staff; insurance consultants are commissioned	Branch staff paid on salary only

Success of entry	Not many tangible benefits from merger so far	Black Horse very successful, Abbey Life less successful. Synergy effects between the two subsidiaries yet elusive	Sales rates so far disappointing. No tangible benefits of merger up to present

It becomes apparent that the predominant motive for engaging in a merger or an acquisition was to reap the benefits of synery effects. Establishing actual benefits in practice has turned out to be difficult, however, as integration problems have been numerous and the strive for synergy has proven to be a difficult process. As integrating two companies in a merger or an acquisition is a time-consuming process, however, it may be too early to assess the transactions in conclusion.

6. Key success factors for banks entering insurance: lessons from the case studies

This final section pursues two main objectives: first, it presents the main conclusions and lessons which can be drawn from a comparative analysis of the case studies. Second, it expands and elaborates on some of the issues which have emerged as critical in the case studies and develop these further, incorporating the existing theoretical and empirical literature in management studies.

I identify three main issues which are crucial for banks' entry strategies into insurance. First, the question whether any particular entry vehicle has advantages over its strategic alternatives. Second, the issue of market segmentation and related marketing and distribution approaches. Finally, the question of how to reconcile different payment systems which exist within the banking and insurance cultures and how to design an effective incentive system for retail financial services distribution.

6.1. Pros and cons of alternative entry vehicles: is there an optimal entry route?

The previous section has presented case studies of the four different entry vehicles which a bank has when entering insurance. This section provides a comparative analysis of the four entry vehicles to analyse and compare the relative success of each entry route.

6.1.1. De novo entry

The case studies of de novo entries of the four selected banks document an astonishing success rate. In fact, whenever success stories of bancassurance are cited, it is most commonly one of the case studies which the previous section discussed. Which factors explain this high success rate of de novo entries?

First and perhaps most importantly, when entering insurance via de novo entry banks enjoy the greatest degree of *strategic flexibility*. This implies that they are able to design a tailored entry strategy into insurance which best suits their specific competitive environment and internal structure. Thus, a bank can systematically build on its specific strengths and fully exploit potential synergy effects. In addition, banks also enjoy a significant degree of organizational freedom concerning the introduction of insurance products into the banking culture. There is no need to amalgamate a new corporate culture such as in a merger or an acquisition and a different sales culture can be gradually infused into the organization rather than by shock therapy. A distribution approach can be chosen which optimises the strengths of the organization and takes account of the historical evolution of the specific corporate culture.

Thus, possibly the most significant advantage of de novo entry is that it allows a tailored solution to the idiosyncratic situation of the bank. Unlike for a co-operative venture or an acquisition, no compromises need to be struck and bank management has full control over its distribution approach and can design a marketing and distribution approach as well as an incentive structure in a way which best suits its own corporate culture and specific operating environment. In addition, management can build on a wealth of experience about entry moves by other firms and can apply the lessons learned in a careful study of industry dynamics and customer needs.

De novo entry may have the main disadvantage that management starts low on the learning curve. The concept of the learning curve has received wide-spread popularity in the management literature and consultancies such as the Boston Consulting Group have placed considerable emphasis on its strategic significance. The concept of learning was incorporated early into economic theory with Arrow's analysis of learning effects (1962). The concept is based on the observation that unit costs decrease, the longer a firm has been active in a particular market.[9] Such a decrease in unit costs may be the result of several forces at work. Management acquires better know-how about market and industry conditions and critical success factors and can therefore adjust its strategy accordingly. Production and sales personnel accumulate experience and become more efficient in handling day-to-day processes. As different marketing, organizational and production techniques are probed, the firm is likely to move closer to the optimal mix and is able to reduce operating costs and maximise revenues. It should therefore be noted that learning effects do not only convey a competitive advantage in terms of costs but also help to increase revenues for a firm which has been operating in the market for a period of time.

Learning effects do not always convey a competitive advantage, however, as there is a balance between a first-mover advantage in terms of gaining market share and establishing a reputation on the one hand, and the costs incurred when preparing the market for a new product, on the other hand. Thus, it may be the case that first-mover advantages outweigh the costs of starting low on the learning curve.

As was seen in the case studies, one way to reduce resulting problems stemming from lack of know-how is to recruit experienced personnel or engage consultants which have long-standing experience in the industry. In particular, appointing an insurance expert to an executive position can help to instill the required 'insurance' spirit into the organization.

A comparative analysis of the cases illustrates that there is no dominant paradigm which could constitute a standard 'recipe' for de novo entry into insurance. Nevertheless, there are some common threads which characterise the cases studied. While all banks which distribute insurance via regular branch employees have chosen a range of simple products in order not to overextend the distributional skills of their front-line sales employees, other banks have introduced insurance counsellors in the branches. One could therefore hypothesise that there is an evolution of the distribution approach from simple products which can still be distributed via banking employees to a more sophisticated product range which requires specialised skills of a designated insurance counsellor. Such an evolutionary model would reflect the experience of both TSB which started with selling life insurance via branch employees as well as Deutsche Bank's which introduced designated insurance counsellors.

De novo entry has the additional advantage that there is no need to pay costly commissions to sales staff since insurance is introduced into a banking culture and there are no expectations to be compensated by additional commissions. Thus, none of the banks studied pay a significant amount of commission to their branch banking employees which would be comparable to that of an insurance agent.

It becomes clear from a comparative analysis of the case studies that every bank has chosen a unique approach which best suits its organizational and market environment. It is exactly this strategic flexibility which constitutes the most significant advantage of de novo entry.

6.1.2. Strategic distribution alliances and joint ventures

Why does a firm choose a co-operative venture rather than de novo entry or a merger or an acquisition? Frequently, they are formed with the strategic goal of combining complementary skills or assets of the two co-operating partners (e.g. Balakrishnan and Koza, 1989). The resulting formation is expected to be more likely to succeed than if the two partners were to expand through internal or market transaction. Thus, the strategic rationale of co-operative agreements can be summarised with the simple statement that "one plus one should equal more than two".

Frequently, the main motive for entering a co-operative alliance rather than forming a de novo unit is the perceived need of rapidly acquiring know-how which would otherwise have to be built up in a time-consuming process. In particular, in situations where a firm needs to catch up quickly with other market participants which have already acquired the requisite know-how, co-operative ventures are a way of pooling expertise and making up for the time gap which has arisen between the market leader and firms which enter subsequently.

In addition, co-operative ventures have the advantage that capital needs are usually significantly lower than for the case of either de novo entry or acquisition. Thus, especially medium-sized firms which often have fewer capital resources find a co-operative venture attractive in terms of its potential return on capital employed.

Another possible motive for a co-operative venture is that two firms may want to expand their sales power by pooling distribution networks. In theory, if both networks were fully compatible and products were mutually distributed such pooling may lead to a doubling of sales.

In practice, however, strategic distribution alliances appear to be less successful than de novo entries, resulting from a number of practical obstacles which prevent success and may even lead to negative effects when attempting to reap the benefits of synergy effects.

Which theoretical reasons can explain this lack of success? At the core of any co-operative agreement is a more or less formalised long-term contract which may be explicit or implicit detailing the strategic objectives and its operational implementation concerning product and distribution approach as well as incentive structures. Such long-term contracts are frequently subject to inherent instability, however, since partners may interpret them in a way which is to their best advantage and display opportunistic behaviour in the course of a changing environment or when altering strategic positions (Williamson, 1989; Klein, Crawford and Alchian, 1978).

Another source of potential problems of co-operative ventures in the context of bancassurance is that strategic intents of banks and insurers may diverge. As is noted by Lorange and Ross (1992, p. 12-13), one of the key factors of success in a co-operative venture is that

> the prospective partners must negotiate a joint understanding of how their resource perspectives and strategy perspectives can be reconciled ... A significant mismatch in the positions of the two parties would make it unrealistic to form, implement, and evolve any type of strategic alliance.

In the context of bancassurance, it may be the case that the strategic intents of the co-operating bank and insurer are not compatible. For example, while an insurer -traditionally sales and commission-oriented- may want to maximise its sales through the bank's branch network to reap the highest possible commissions, a bank may place greater emphasis on counselling and delivering the financial solution which best satisfies the customer's needs. Thus, rather than selling the product with the highest commission, a bank may stress that branch employees should tailor their sales recommendations to the customer's specific needs in order to secure the long-term customer relationship.

For these reasons, co-operative ventures are likely to be successful only when strategies of firms are compatible, both firms contribute and profit from the venture in about equal proportions and co-operation promises to have a long-term potential. In the context of bancassurance, these conditions are likely to be fulfilled only for a very limited number of cases. For the majority of cases it therefore appears that co-operative ventures in bancassurance are characterised by a number of operational and implementation problems stemming from diverging strategic intents of its participants.

Empirical studies of co-operative ventures across a range of industries seem to confirm these theoretical arguments, as they frequently find disappointing results with unsatisfactory outcomes ranging from 40 per cent to 70 per cent of the analysed ventures (e.g. Mariti and Smiley, 1983; Reynolds and Snapp, 1986; Beamish, 1987; Harrigan, 1986; Kogut, 1989a, b).

Simply adding insurance products on top of banking products in the branch network does not suffice to achieve an adequate incentive for bank employees to proactively sell these products. As the example of Dresdner Bank illustrates, branch employees need more than a small financial incentive to actively distribute insurance products of the co-operating partner. A careful incentive and training scheme must therefore be implemented to increase the degree of employee identification with insurance products.

It appears easier to adapt the bank branch to insurance distribution than the insurance sales network to bank products. This stems from the fact that banking is usually characterised by more frequent interaction between customer and branch employee due to the large number of transactions connected with accounts, loans and investment decisions. Insurance distribution, on the other hand, is mostly characterised by one-off sales with less-frequent claims handling and a low degree of personal involvement on the part of the insurance agent. As a result, banks have a comparative advantage in distribution due to the higher frequency of customer interaction. In addition, they also enjoy reputational advantages over insurers, since customers frequently perceive insurers as 'hard sellers', whereas banks have traditionally positioned themselves as 'financial counsellors' acting in the customer's best interest. Thus, in a mutual distribution alliance insurers have more to gain from using the bank's retail branch network, while banks find it more difficult to distribute their products through an insurer's sales network. In addition, banks are likely to learn quickly from co-operating with an insurer and thereby acquire the required know-how and expertise to run an insurance business independently. As a result of these factors, co-operative ventures between banks and insurers are unlikely to be stable in the long run, since banks have an incentive to buy out their joint venture partner or to terminate the distribution alliance, once they have acquired the necessary insurance know-how.

In comparison to a strategic distribution alliance, joint ventures provide a clearer organizational structure of the co-operation between a bank and an insurer. Distribution and incentive systems must be clearly defined and there is a tangible degree of organizational commitment to the entry move into insurance.

The case studies have shown that the precise organizational structure of a joint venture can vary significantly. However, in all ventures banks play a dominating role in terms of shareholding of the joint venture. In addition, there appears to be a trend that banks increase their stake in the joint venture, once a sufficient know-how base is established. Thus, the main motive for entering a joint venture with an insurer seems to be to leapfrog their know-how base. This stems from the fact that banks own the most significant asset of the joint venture which is the retail franchise. Thus, once insurers have contributed their know-how to the joint venture, they seem to have little further to contribute. Accordingly they are bought out by the bank, unless they themselves acquire a stake in the bank as in the case of Standard Life and Bank of Scotland.

In effect, joint ventures are therefore a mechanism for banks to quickly acquire a know-how base for insurance. However, they do not appear to be stable organizational forms since they frequently end up with the acquisition of the joint venture by the bank.

6.1.3. Mergers and acquisitions

Mergers and acquisitions provide the potential of combining banking and insurance know-how in one organization. At the same time, they may pose significant integration problems (e.g. Mueller, 1989; Ravenscraft and Scherer, 1987, 89). For any acquisition there are adjustment costs which inexorably arise and which need to be compared to those costs occurring for a de novo entry. Such costs result, for example, from the fact that insurance products may have to be re-designed to suit the requirements of a branch-based distribution channel. In many instances, de novo entry provides for more flexibility in designing new products and tailoring products and distribution approach towards the specific situation of the bank.

Caves (1982) notes that acquisitions carry a lower potential return than de novo entry. This stems from the fact that the market for company acquisitions is near-efficient, where firms which are for sale are valued and priced according to their future earning potential. Thus, there are unlikely to be 'bargains' in the market for company acquisitions which stems from the fact that there are always several bidders for a firm for sale and the seller therefore has the possibility to engage potential buyers in a race of competitive bidding. As a result, acquisitions may well be overpriced in particular in situations where several bidders have driven up the price to levels well-above a realistic estimate of the net present value of the target firm. The firm which comes first in competitive race to acquire a company may therefore be subject to 'winner's curse', a well-known result from auction theory (e.g. Maskin and Riley, 1985; Milgrom, 1987). Winner's curse refers to the fact that, as a result of the process of competitive bidding, the 'winner' in an auction may be paying a price which exceeds the inherent value of the good to be acquired.

Caves also argues that acquisitions are characterised by lower risk than de novo entry. In the context of bancassurance, one may have doubts whether this claim holds true, however, since de novo entry usually involves a significantly lower investment outlay than an acquisition and therefore a lower write-off in case of failure. In addition, acquisitions are frequently characterised by asymmetric information where the buyer has imperfect knowledge concerning the true value of the target firm's assets and business potential. Thus, it is not uncommon that acquiring firms are faced with unpleasant surprises after the takeover since previously unknown liabilities may surface and asset quality is not nearly as good as was estimated before the takeover.

Another frequent problem with acquisitions is an overoptimistic assessment of potential synergy effects between the acquiring firm and the target (e.g. Adolf, Cramer and Ollman, 1991). Such overestimation frequently stems from the need to justify the acquisition price to shareholders and the capital market in order to convey the impression that the acquisition promises significant advantages and will benefit the share price. Thus, as argued above, synergy effects may be significant in theory, but in practice management may find it hard to reap predicted benefits once the task of implementation starts. Ennew, Wong and Wright (1992, p. 480), for example, note that

a major obstacle encountered by acquirers is their ability to integrate the different cultures and management styles of the parent company with those of the newly purchased subsidiary, which may induce harmful resistance to change and prevent potential merger benefits from being fully realised.

A particular problem in the context of bancassurance is that of blending two possibly very different corporate cultures linked to banking on the one hand and insurance on the other (e.g. Schneider, 1988).[10] Such a difference stems from the fact that insurance is usually sales and commission-driven, whereas banking has traditionally been less sales-oriented. Linking these two different sales cultures may lead to clashes at all levels of the organization.

At the top management level, for example, both sides in a merger of equals may attempt to secure a dominant position and not be willing to give up acquired influence. Thus, rather than co-operating, the board may spend a significant amount of time and energy bargaining about stakes and power positions.

Similarly, at the branch level there may be a conflict due to different compensation systems, since insurance agents are traditionally paid on a commission-basis, whereas banking staff are usually salary-based. As insurance staff can therefore reach significantly higher levels of earnings, there may be jealousies and potential antagonistic behaviour between the two groups, threatening the overall success of the merger or acquisition.

As the example of Lloyds Abbey Life shows, it is especially difficult to integrate an insurance sales network into a banking culture. Many of the synergy benefits which Lloyds Abbey Life realised from the merger could also have been achieved by setting up Black Horse Financial Services as a joint venture which would have constituted a similar degree of organizational commitment.

Mergers may also be fraught with difficulties due to resistance from an insurer's indigenous sales network, as shown by the example of Internationale Nederlanden Group. Sales agents naturally fear the competition of the bank branch as a less costly distribution channel and may therefore try to torpedo the success of the merger or attempt to place pressure on the insurer. However, if the bank does not employ its retail branch network as a distribution channel then the main strategic rationale of the merger is undermined, thus jeopardising the success of the whole entry move.

In summary, mergers and acquisitions may therefore pose a range of problems for banks which choose this entry route into insurance and it appears a difficult task to reap the full potential of synergy effects between banking and insurance.[11]

To summarise the main insights concerning the choice of the entry vehicle drawn from the case studies, it appears that one of the fundamental prerequisites for successful entry of a bank into insurance is a high level of organizational and cultural integration between banking and insurance. As this section argued, such co-operation appears difficult to achieve for distribution alliances. To a lesser extent this also applies to joint ventures. Mergers and acquisitions on the other hand, bring with them a range of integration problems and synergy effects turn out to be difficult to achieve. Thus, it appears that de novo entry promises to be the most successful entry route for banks wishing to enter the insurance market.

6.2. Customer segmentation and distribution approach to bancassurance

6.2.1. Recognising customer needs for successful segmentation

One of the key requirements for banks when entering insurance is to determine the needs of customers and classify specific customer groups into market segments.

Why is customer segmentation so important in the area of bancassurance? Firstly, segmentation provides a potentially powerful tool to better recognise and serve customer needs and thereby create a competitive advantage over rivals (Smith, 1956).[12] In particular, customer segmentation allows targeting and tailoring of marketing and distribution approach towards the specific needs of a particular customer group. Secondly, as was stressed by several executives in the personal interviews which I conducted, life insurance is a product which "does not sell itself" but where the bank actively needs to approach the customer. In order to do so, the bank requires a convincing selling proposition to raise the customer's interest and convey the need for purchasing life insurance to the client.

According to Kotler (1991, p. 278), effective segmentation requires fulfilling four basic criteria:

- *measurability*, i.e. the segmentation criterion needs to be quantifiable when applying it to the target market;
- *substantiality* referring to the fact that segments need to be of sufficiently large size and importance to make them worthwhile to target;
- *accessibility*, referring to the extent that segments can be reached and targeted through means of communication;
- *actionability* which means that marketing programs based on a particular way of segmentation need to be executable given the specific firm's environment and resources.

In addition to these four criteria, a fifth criterion, *operationality*, seems useful which refers to the fact that when increasing the number of segments there is a trade-off between being able to fine-tune marketing and distribution efforts and administering organizational complexity which arises from an increased number of segments requiring individual administration. Thus, there are likely to be decreasing returns when increasing the number of segments beyond a certain optimal number, since organizational and administrative complexity makes segmentation unwieldy. In practice, most banks seem to settle for a number of segments between two (e.g. Dresdner Bank) and seven (e.g. Rabobank). For the purpose of segmenting life insurance customers it appears that identifying only two segments is not sufficient for effectively recognising customer needs. This stems from the fact that segmentation in life insurance is usually at least two-dimensional with age and income constituting two crucial criteria. Age is significant as it determines the type and contract length of the life insurance product, whereas rising income usually correlates with an increasing demand for private retirement provision as the gap between public provision and the attained standard of living increases.[13]

Once the market has been segmented, a bank needs to determine whether it wants to service all or only a subset of segments. In general, even when a firm decides to service all segments, it has to identify which of the segments has the greatest business potential so that it can focus its marketing resources appropriately. A crucial question in this context is being able to identify the profit potential of each customer. In order to do so on a cost-effective basis, adequate information technology support constitutes a necessary prerequisite for both effective segmentation as well as identification of customer potential.

Compared to other financial institutions such as insurers, for example, banks have the significant strategic advantage that they can access a wide range of data about their customers. This stems from the long-term relationship which most customers have with their bank. Information which can be gathered from bank data usually includes not only current address, occupation, date of birth and family status, but also employment status, wealth and even income data which can be derived from an analysis of payment streams on the current account. Thus, this powerful source of information concerning the customer can provide the basis for an effective segmentation strategy. In addition to such 'hard' data, bank officials can find out additional 'soft' data concerning risk preference or financing wishes, for example, in personal interviews with the customer. In order to be able to organise and effectively analyse this wealth of information, a database is required which allows data segmentation and stratification on a personalised in addition to an account or product-based level. As became apparent in the interviews, however, few banks currently possess such a database system which allows effective segmentation, since banks' information systems were traditionally product-oriented rather than customer-oriented.

6.2.2. Distributional modes of integrating insurance services into the bank branch

One of the main issues in bancassurance concerns the distributional approach which the bank chooses to service its customers with insurance products. Two main approaches can be distinguished:

- the *integrative* approach: insurance products are sold directly by branch staff which have received training in insurance selling techniques and product requirements.
- the *specialist* approach: an insurance specialist serves bank customers inside the branch and may also visit them outside branch opening hours. He or she receives systematic referrals from branch staff.

There are also several intermediate forms which combine elements of both the specialist and the integrative approach. For example, as part of a basically integrative approach, certain branch staff may acquire some specific know-how on insurance products so that they would become quasi-specialists without devoting all their time to selling insurance as in the full-specialist approach.

Both distribution approaches have pros and cons. The specialist approach has the advantage that an insurance sales agent can devote all his time to selling insurance products. Thus, he is able to build up special expertise and know-how required in this area and draw on a wide wealth of experience. Due to the fact that the total number of products sold by the insurance consultant is lower than for a branch employee, training can be more intense and better-focused on this area. At the same time, an insurance specialist may have a higher standing with the customer who places a greater degree of trust into a specialist and feels better-advised than when being served by regular branch staff.

On the other hand, creating a separate position for an insurance specialist may lead to a hiatus between regular branch staff and the insurance agent and result in a lower degree of co-operation and cross-referral rate. Such problems are most likely to occur when the insurance specialist is compensated on a different basis than her retail banking colleagues. The following section will further address this problem of introducing different compensation systems into the banking environment.

From the case studies it appears that the specialist approach is preferred by banks which introduce more complicated insurance products. Only if products are sufficiently simple, standardised and few in number does the integrative approach appear to be successful such as in the case of Crédit Agricole, for example. TSB, Deutsche Bank and BNP all have changed their distribution approach from integrative to specialist, as product and distribution requirements increased in complexity and imposed greater demands on regular bank staff.

In addition to deciding on whether to adopt a specialist or an integrative distribution approach, a bank needs to decide whether different customer segments should be served by means of a differentiated distribution channel. Such differentiation could consist, for example, of appointing specialist customer advisers for different segments. As was seen in the case studies, a number of banks which have stratified their customer base according to income also pursue different distributional strategies. A large German bank, for example, introduced two types of advisers in its branches. Advisers for lower-income customers serve on average 1,500 customers, whereas advisers for the higher-income group have a customer base of only around 300 customers. The strategic rationale for such differentiation is that high-income customers have a higher profit potential for the bank and that therefore the consultation process requires a longer period of time than for low-income customers. The bank had found that in retail financial services it earned 80 per cent of its total income from only 20 per cent of its customer base and that bank profits per customer were closely correlated to personal income. As a result, it was decided to dedicate a separate distribution channel to higher-income customers rather than serving all customers via the same channel.

The implication of such differentiation of distribution channels according to income for integrating insurance into the banking environment is that insurance products for lower-income customers need to be characterised by a higher degree of standardisation, since customer advisers have less time to spend with each customer.

In summary, it appears that retail financial services will be increasingly characterised by distributional fine-tuning, as banks have recognised that different customer groups and market segments can be better served by dedicated distribution channels (e.g. Gapper, 1993b). This trend will not leave banks' strategies in insurance unaffected, with specialisation according to customer segments increasingly likely to determine both marketing and distribution approach.

6.3. Devising an effective incentive structure for bancassurance

One of the fundamental issues in bancassurance is that of determining an efficient incentive structure for branch staff once insurance products are introduced into the organization. This stems from the fact that the structure of compensation is quite different in the banking and insurance sectors. While retail banking employees are normally rewarded on a fixed salary basis with 'time worked' being the basis of compensation, insurance agents work mostly on a commission basis dependent upon sales performance. Thus, a bank which enters insurance is faced with the decision problem of whether to introduce commission-based compensation, i.e. performance-contingent pay into the organization or whether to maintain its salary-focused structure.

The following section provides a critical review of the literature on pay for performance systems, while focusing more specifically on the area of bancassurance in section 6.3.2.

6.3.1. *Payment systems and incentives: a review of the literature*

Pay for performance is usually defined as the explicit and immediate link of compensation to individual or group performance. The area has recently enjoyed a revival of interest in organizational behaviour theory and practice.[14] Nevertheless, it is not as well-researched as other areas of organizational behaviour. As Hopkins (1992, p. 4) notes, for example, "little is known about pay in a hard and fast way. Even experts understand little about how effectively to use pay." This section therefore provides a critical review of the main issues arising in the context of pay for performance systems.

When differentiating pay for performance systems, two main approaches can be distinguished. First, group-based schemes provide financial incentives to a collection of employees which work in a group. In the banking context, such a group would typically consist of a branch, for example. Second, individualised schemes relate to individual performance and can be based either on qualitative assessments of the individual employee or link pay to an objectively quantifiable variable such as level of sales. When payment is linked to qualitative assessments such a scheme is referred to as a merit-based system, whereas a link based on clearly quantifiable data is termed a piece-rate system.

What are the objectives of introducing pay for performance into an organization? First and foremost, organizations introducing such schemes frequently aim at improving motivation of employees and thus productivity in sales or manufacturing by inducing employees to maximise efforts (e.g. Armstrong and Murlis, 1991, p. 211). In order to understand the possible impact of pay for performance on employee motivation, some of the basic concepts of motivation theory need to be introduced. This section therefore provides a brief review of these theories.[15]

In the context of organizational behaviour, Wright (1987) defines motivation as "the willingness to expend effort on a particular task in order to attain an incentive or incentives of a certain type". Since the use of the term "incentive" is somewhat misleading in this definition, I prefer to define employee motivation as "the willingness to expend effort on a particular task to attain a certain intrinsic or extrinsic objective".

Two main groups of theory can be distinguished addressing the issue of motivation. First, *content* theories of motivation are mainly concerned with the concept of 'need' and the factors which induce motivation. *Process* theories, on the other hand, primarily analyse how specific forces impact the concrete form in which motivated behaviour manifests itself. I will discuss both theories in turn.

Content theories of motivation go back to F.W. Taylor (1903, 1911), the founder of "scientific management". Taylor believed that monetary rewards were crucial for inducing the optimal level of motivation and that designing an appropriate wage incentive scheme based on a careful job description and time and motion studies would significantly increase productivity.[16] While empirical studies largely confirmed such an increase in productivity (e.g. Lawler, 1971), researchers had realised early on that monetary rewards are not the only factor motivating behaviour.[17]

This view seemed to be empirically confirmed in what has probably become one of the most famous experiments in organizational behaviour: the Hawthorne studies. These experiments were conducted between 1927 and 1932 in a manufacturing plant of Western Electric Company in Illinois and consisted of analysing the impact of different incentive schemes and changing working conditions on worker productivity.[18] A curious phenomenon was described by the researchers accompanying the experiments: in the Relay Assembly Room rest pauses, lighting and work duration were changed in consultation with the workers and, as a result, productivity increased. However, when work conditions were set back to their original state productivity increased again. This observation which was later termed the "Hawthorne effect" seemed to indicate that it was not the changes in working conditions *per se* which increased productivity but the fact that workers were given special attention and subjected to an experimental situation which influenced their behaviour. This result provided strong evidence that monetary incentives are not the sole factor influencing worker motivation and productivity, as a narrow interpretation of scientific management may have suggested.[19] As a response to the Hawthorne experiments, researchers therefore developed multidimensional models of explaining the driving forces of human behaviour of which Maslow's "hierarchy of needs" (1943) is probably the best-known example.

While such content theories of motivation provide a useful starting point for analysing human needs, these theories cannot tell us how motivated behaviour actually manifests itself in human behaviour. In order to better understand the link between a human need and actual manifested behaviour, a theory of the *process* of motivation is required. The most important strand among such process theories is that of expectancy theory (Vroom, 1964; Porter and Lawler, 1968). This theory holds that motivation is impacted by two variables, value of rewards and effort-reward expectations. Value of rewards refers to the preference ordering of the individual concerning possible outcomes. These may be either extrinsic when they derive from the social environment of the individual or intrinsic if they derive from inside the individual. Effort-reward expectations, on the other hand, refer to the probability that rewards will result from a particular effort. Thus, phrased in the parlance of expectancy theory, linking financial compensation directly to performance will lead to greater motivation only if monetary rewards figure prominently as value of rewards of the individual and if there is a clear expectational link between performance and rewards.

A second objective to introduce pay for performance systems may be to gain a competitive edge over rivals in terms of recruiting, employee retention and selection. Competitive advantages in recruiting and employees retention may arise if employees find pay for performance more attractive than regular payment systems and therefore prefer to work for a firm which offers such a payment structure. However, such a strategic advantage will only be maintained as long as the firm occupies an innovative position in the area of payment systems. Employee selection occurs as employees who do not meet performance targets and therefore receive a lower income than the average decide to leave the organization.[20]

A third objective of pay for performance systems is to introduce a greater degree of fairness into the organization where better-performing employees are rewarded with higher pay. Thus, employees are paid according to their contributions and 'free-riders' are penalised by lower pay. As Moss Kanter (1989, p. 234) notes, "there is a strongly held belief that performance-based reward not only is fairer, but also encourages higher levels of productivity, as people learn that they will get back more if they put in more".

Fourthly, it is argued that introducing pay for performance schemes can lead to a change in the corporate culture, shifting the organizational focus to become more sales-oriented, for example (Schien, 1985). This stems from the fact that altering the payment structure sends a clear signal to employees that individual performance is given greater importance in the organization.

Despite these potential advantages of pay for performance systems, relatively few companies have so far adopted performance-related compensation schemes with the notable exception of the sales area where compensation has traditionally been on a performance-related scale. What explains this slow dissemination of an apparently good idea?

The hesitation on the part of many companies to adopt performance-contingent compensation systems stems at least partly from practical implementation problems concerning the actual design and operation of such a scheme. As Armstrong and Murlis (1991, p. 212) note, "recent research has taught us ... that badly designed and poorly implemented performance-related pay schemes will demotivate staff probably more successfully than well-designed and implemented schemes will motivate them."

Two main factors explain why pay for performance may not have the desired effects. First, a forceful conceptual argument against contingent payment systems frequently put forward by organizational psychologists is that the focus on extrinsic monetary rewards may overshadow intrinsic motivation. This claim originally derived from child psychology where providing monetary rewards for good school performance is widely considered to be detrimental to childrens' intrinsic motivation such as the joy of learning and exploring (e.g. Lepper *et al.*, 1973). In an analogous manner, it is argued that providing monetary rewards for employee performance may lead to an usurpation of other motivating factors such as self-actualisation or esteem needs.[21] Thus, monetary rewards for specific functions or tasks may induce employees to complete a task as quickly as possible to maximise incentive payments, resulting in a lower quality of work.[22] In addition, employees when 'controlled' by an incentive scheme may not feel as the master of their own fate but feel steered from outside which may lead to sub-optimal performance.[23] Behaviourists have doubted the basic premise of these theories, however, as they disclaim the existence of an inherent conflict between intrinsic and extrinsic motivation (e.g. Mawhinney *et al.*, 1989). In contrast, they do not see any basic incompatibility between extrinsic and intrinsic rewards and claim that external rewards supplement rather than substitute intrinsic motivation. In particular in the context of the work place it appears that there is unlikely to be a basic conflict between intrinsic and extrinsic motivation. However, performance-related schemes, when not designed correctly, may provide the wrong incentives to employees and the next section will return to this issue when discussing applications to the issue of bancassurance.

A second argument against merit-based pay refers to the fact that such schemes are unlikely to be successful unless employees believe that the assessment of their work is undertaken in an objective and fair way. If this is not the case then, in the

parlance of expectancy theory, effort-reward expectations will
be adjusted downward.

Concerning empirical evidence on pay for performance,
Thierry (1987) reviews the research on payment systems and
notes that for merit-based systems unfavourable outcomes were
reported for 13 out of 14 cases. Reasons for this dismal performance were lack of clarity linking pay to performance, differences in bonus payments being too small to form a sufficient incentive and the fact that the time gap in performance and rewards was too long. In contrast, piece-rate systems were
ranked as favourable in 44 instances and only 3 cases of unfavourable results were reported.

Moss Kanter (1987, p. 233-38) also describes powerful evidence that merit-based systems have led to dismal and even
dysfunctional results due to a range of practical implementation
problems. She concludes that merit-based pay is "one of those
apparently good ideas that doesn't really work as intended"
(1987, p. 233). As one of the main problems, she cites the fact
that, in practice, evaluation of employees is fraud with problems,
since it creates social problems including conflicts between peers
as well as employees and supervisors. Similarly, Cannel and
Wood (1992, p. 27) note that "in terms of culture, encourage-
ment of co-operation, achievement of high standards, and the
extension and flexible use of skills, individual payment by results
schemes provide no advantage and can even be harmful".

The next section discusses a possible solution to the pay for
performance dilemma in the specific context of bancassurance.

6.3.2. Incentive structures in the context of bancassurance

Bank employees have traditionally been compensated on a
salary basis. Typically, an employee starts out on a basic salary
which is more or less equal for all employees with a similar kind
of work experience at the same hierarchical and functional level.
Salary increases are dependent on the number of years which
the employee spends with the organization, her age and her
performance on the job which can result in promotions and a
rise in the hierarchy. Individual employee performance thus influences compensation on a medium- or even long-term basis,
rather than being immediately tangible in the monthly pay
cheque.

Insurance agents, in contrast, are usually compensated on a commission-basis with either no basic salary at all or only a very low base salary. Thus, their financial rewards crucially depend on their success of selling policies.

In the context of bancassurance, a bank therefore faces the basic decision problem of whether to maintain its current salary structure or to introduce a more performance-oriented pay structure when incorporating insurance products into the organization.[24]

From the case studies it becomes apparent that most banks have basically adopted a salary-dominated structure with a small commission element attached which is awarded according to performance. The fact that few banks have introduced a more performance-oriented pay structure results from a number of arguments which were frequently put forward by executives in the personal interviews which I conducted:

- pay for performance may induce selling which focuses on products with the greatest commissions rather than recommending the product portfolio which is in the customer's best interest and is therefore incompatible with the traditional banking culture;
- introducing performance-related pay unilaterally only for insurance sales agents may lead to inequalities between retail banking and insurance staff and causes clashes between two different selling cultures;
- personalised pay for performance systems may discourage team work and encourage individualistic behaviour, thus reducing the scope for individuals to become team players in the branch;
- pay for performance may increase personnel costs, since above-average performers are rewarded, whereas below-average performers are usually not penalised.

I will argue that these arguments do not apply when a group-based pay for performance system is introduced where many of the problems of merit-based systems can be avoided.

Piecerate systems which would be the alternative to a merit-based system could also be introduced in the context of bancassurance where insurance sales staff would be compensated on a commission-based level. However, it appears that for the specialist approach compensating insurance staff on a commission level may lead to conflicts between the branches' bank staff and insurance sales staff, since the latter can reach substantially higher earnings than bank employees. Thus, there is the potential of jealousies and rivalries which may threaten the successful co-operation between bank and insurance sales staff which is crucial for the overall success of entry into insurance. For the integrative approach a piecerate system is likely to lead to an unjustified favouring of insurance products over other banking products unless all products are commissioned. In addition, piecerate systems create problems of apportioning the customer base between individual customer advisers and encourage competitive behaviour and rivalry rather than team-building in the branch.

In contrast, a group-based system has the advantages that it encourages team work in the organization and provides a natural incentive to co-operate closely to maximise the branch's performance.[25]

Group incentive schemes usually suffer from the weakness that, in practice, it is hard to identify the proper social group which should be the smallest basis for such a scheme. In retail banking, however, the branch constitutes a clear-cut unit of organization. Thus, a pay for performance scheme can centre around the branch as the basic unit of linking pay to performance.

Several different measures for branch performance are conceivable but the most widely used is that of the contribution margin which is calculated as total revenues (i.e. interest and commission income) less costs which are directly attributable to the branch (thus excluding costs of maintaining headquarters, for example).

Introducing a branch-based incentive system has the additional advantage that it does not favour insurance products over banking products in its incentive structure which could lead to disparities between the product sectors. There is no obvious reason why only insurance products should be rewarded on a commission-level. Rather, the introduction of insurance products should be used as an opportunity to introduce a more performance-oriented pay structure for the whole branch network.

Perhaps the greatest advantage of a group-based system is that it encourages team building. The significance of effective team work has recently received renewed interest in the management literature (e.g. Katzenbach and Smith, 1992, 1993).

Working in groups is one of the central features of organizational behaviour.[26] Baron (1986, p. 240) defines a group as

a collection of two or more interacting individuals with a stable pattern of relationships between them who share common goals and who perceive themselves as being a group.

Teams, in contrast, are defined as

a small number of people with complementary skills who are committed to a common purpose, performance goals, and approach for which they hold themselves mutually responsible" (Katzenbach and Smith, 1992, p. 5).

Groups and teams thus differ in four respects:
• First, teams are characterised by the fact that members have complementary skills. In the context of bancassurance, this could imply, for example, that branch employees develop specific areas of expertise with some staff specialising on certain products.
• Second, teams need to be committed to a common purpose and performance goals rather than just sharing common goals. This implies that there needs to be a clearly defined mission such as "providing the best available service to customers" and measurable objectives which could consist, for example, of a specified target contribution margin of the branch which could be further broken down into specific sales targets and cross-referral rates.
• Third, teams need to commit to a common working approach. This requires that job descriptions and tasks are clearly defined and that decision structures and skill profiles are determined.
• Finally, team members need to be mutually accountable which requires that each member shares responsibilities and takes a stake in the team's overall performance.

How does a group-based performance-linked compensation scheme assist the team-building effort? First, it requires a clearly defined and quantifiable target to which compensation of branch employees can be linked. Such targets could consist of high customer satisfaction, as measured by customer surveys, for example, or of specific sales targets. In addition, a group-based compensation system helps to reduce intra-team rivalries between members, since it links pay to team rather than individual performance. As a result, team members have an incentive to co-operate and maximise the benefits from exploiting complementary skills. Working in a team can provide a powerful motivational stimulus to firm employees. As noted by Berry, Parasuraman and Zeithaml (1992, p. 229), for example, "team participation can unleash one of the most potent of motivators - the respect of peers". Since a team is characterised by the fact that its overall performance exceeds that of the sum of individual contributions, a group-based system provides the right incentive structure for team members and team leader -the branch manager- to structure team processes and skills in a way which maximise overall performance. In particular, if the specialist approach is chosen for insurance distribution, rewarding overall branch performance rather than sales performance of specific employees or products encourages close co-operation between banking employees and insurance agents. Since cross-referrals are crucial for the success of the bancassurance venture, a branch-based compensation scheme therefore constitutes a potentially powerful incentive for maximising a joint utility function rather than individual utilities.

A frequent argument against a branch-based compensation system is that it does not take sufficient account of individual performance and does not penalise 'free-riders' who minimise their own work effort but participate in overall team success. It seems likely, however, that such an attempt of 'free-riding' will be quickly discovered by other team members and that peer pressure will induce the free-rider to change his behaviour. If such peer pressure does not succeed the team leader will consider to penalise the free-rider including the possibility of expulsion from the team. As team members know about these possible sanctions, free-riding behaviour is likely to be deterred.

How should compensation be linked to branch performance? It is common for most banks that branches receive annual targets concerning a number of variables such as customer satisfaction, contribution margin, customer acquisition and product sales. These targets are individually determined at the beginning of each year usually between the branch manager and regional branch management and take account of the specific situation of the branch in terms of its customer structure, location, size etc. Compensation of branch employees can then be linked to attaining these specified targets where at least 20 per cent of the total salary should be made dependent on achieving these goals in order to have a sufficient incentive effect. Thus, if the former fixed salary is taken as a base point of 100 per cent then a group-based performance-linked pay system should vary at least in the range of 80 to 120 per cent to provide an adequate motivational stimulus (Smith, 1989).

Overall, it appears that one of the critical success factors for entry into insurance is mobilising the enthusiasm of sales employees. Thus, those organizations which are best able to motivate their employees will gain a competitive advantage in the area of bancassurance. As argued at the beginning of the chapter, this stems from the fact that financial services are characterised by a high degree of employee involvement in the sales process. Thus, it is the front-line employee who "makes or breaks" the sale. This section has argued that a branch-based pay for performance system is likely to constitute a powerful tool for motivating employees.

7. Conclusions

This chapter presented an analysis of how banks enter the insurance sector by analysing thirteen case studies of entry moves of banks. The selected case studies represent the most important examples in European bancassurance and are distributed across each entry vehicle, i.e. de novo entry, strategic distribution alliance, joint venture and merger or acquisition.

A comparative analysis of the different entry vehicles shows that of the four different entry routes, de novo entry seems to be most successful. This stems primarily from the organizational and strategic flexibility which de novo entry offers allowing a tailored solution to the idiosyncratic internal structure and organizational environment of the bank.

Strategic distribution alliances seem to have been least successful, which is mainly due to the lack of a clear incentive structure and identification problems on the part of bank employees with insurance products. Only when there is a significant degree of organizational commitment are distribution alliances more successful.

Joint ventures appear to be relatively more successful than distribution alliances which results from the clearer organizational commitment and management responsibility of the joint venture firm. However, while joint ventures initially pool complementary assets and know-how, they do not seem to be stable in the longer term, since the bank has an incentive to buy out the insurance partner in order to reap a larger part of the profit.

Finally, mergers and acquisitions lead to a range of post-merger problems unless they constitute an evolutionary step in a chain of co-operative modes over a long period of time. Post-merger problems include organizational resistance from inside the firms as well as from the sales network of the insurer which fears the competition posed by the less costly distribution channel of the bank's retail network. The benefit of opening an insurer's sales network to bank products has so far been limited.

In summary, therefore, from an empirical perspective de novo entry has so far been the most successful entry vehicle.

This chapter provided an analysis of two other key factors for success for banks when entering the insurance sector which are marketing approach and establishing an effective incentive system. Concerning the marketing approach, it emphasised that understanding customer needs and effective market segmentation are critical for obtaining a competitive advantage in the area of bancassurance and enumerated criteria for effective market segmentation. In order to gain a competitive advantage compared to insurers, banks need to have an effective information technology system which enables stratification and segmentation of information on a customer- rather than only a product- or account-based level. Concerning the distribution approach of insurance products, the specialist approach, i.e. stationing an insurance specialist in the branch appears superior to the integrative approach, i.e. distributing insurance products through regular branch employees. Only if the insurance product range is kept sufficiently simple as in the case of Credit Agricole, for example, appears the integrative approach to be feasible.

Concerning the issue of establishing an effective incentive system, the traditionally different approaches in banking and insurance present management with a decision problem whether to adopt a more performance-oriented structure or whether to maintain the basic salary approach. I analysed the objectives of pay for performance systems and provided a review of the theoretical and empirical literature. Based on this review, it appears that a branch-based pay for performance system provides the best approach in the area of bancassurance. This stems from the fact that such a system encourages team work and avoids problems of introducing different payment systems side by side in the branch which may jeopardise successful co-operation between banking and insurance staff.

---

1 While recent innovations in the area of direct marketing such as mail correspondence and telephone distribution are likely to reduce the significance of social interaction in retail financial services, the vast majority of services are presently still distributed in a course of face-to-face interaction.

2 In general, marketing has played a relatively insignificant role in financial services for a long time. Ennew *et al.* (1993, p.1) for example, note that "marketing, in the true sense of the word, is relatively new to the financial services sector".

3 For the area of life insurance, for example, George and Myers (1981) find that consumers attach a significant weight to the counselling process and the qualifications and personality of the sales representative.

4 All mergers and acquisitions are included in the final selection of case studies with the exception of CIC-Union Europeene and GAN, as it is an acquisition of a bank by an insurer. All joint ventures are included with the exception of Banque Indosuez, since it is a cross-border joint venture with Spanish Mapfre and is therefore different from domestic joint ventures. All distribution alliances are included with the exception of DG Bank, since it is not a retail bank. Finally, all de novo entries are included with the exception of Paribas, Credit Lyonnais, Societe Generale and Credit Mutuel. These cases were excluded in order to reduce the possibility of a country bias, since with Credit Agricole and BNP (Natio Vie) two French institutions were already included which pursued de novo entries.

5 In addition, keeping the product line manageable reduces the costs of co-ordination and compromise discussed in section 5.5 of part one.

6 This example illustrates Porter's "costs of compromise" discussed in section 5.5 of part one.

7 Another example of a highly successful de novo start-up is that of Lifetime, the life insurance subsidiary of Bank of Ireland, the second-largest Irish bank. Lifetime which started operations in September 1987 achieved 1992 profits of ECU18 million which represented 18 per cent of total group profits. It has achieved a penetration rate of its customer base of around 30

per cent and has a market share of 10 per cent in new non-endowment annual life premiums.

[8] Compare Midland Bank's direct banking subsidiary First Direct founded in 1990 which has so far not reached operating profitability, however, despite a total customer base of more than 400,000.

[9] On the impact of learning by doing on strategic competition see, for example, Spence (1981), Fudenberg and Tirole (1983), Stockey (1986) and Dasgupta and Stiglitz (1988).

[10] As the former chief executive of TSB Trust notes, "be prepared for the clash of cultures ... branch managers and cashiers seldom believe that a life insurance salesperson or a financial services consultant is a reputable person or indeed that a life policy or a unit trust investment is as good a product as a cheque account , a bank deposit or a loan" (Brown, 1992, p.54-55). See Kreps (1990) for a theoretical treatment of the significance of corporate culture.

[11] For further general empirical evidence on mergers and acquisitions see, for example, Cowling *et al.* (1980), Meeks (1977), Hughes, (1989) and Martin (1992).

[12] As Ennew (1990, p.77) notes, for example, "a key element in any process of strategy formulation is market segmentation, the process of identifying and even creating distinct segments within the market to which specific financial services can be targeted". Ennew, Watkins and Wright (1993, p.4) go even one step further and state that understanding customer needs and segmenting the customer franchise constitute the basic prerequisite for any competitive strategy in the financial services field.

[13] See, for example, Speed and Smith (1992) for a comprehensive review of different methods of segmentation in financial services.

[14] As Brady and Wright (1990, p.1), for example, observe: "[performance pay] is one of the most dynamic issues in human resource management and arguably the most topical component of reward policy today".

[15] For a more comprehensive review of theories of motivation see, for example, Weiner (1980), Mitchell (1982) or Kanfer (1990).

[16] See, for example, Peach and Wren (1992) for a historical overview of incentive schemes and pay for performance.

[17] As early as 1920, Williams (1920, p.323), for example, observed that "we give the dollar altogether too great an importance when we consider it the

cause of men's industry ... Beyond a certain point, the increase of wages is quite likely to lessen as to increase effort."

18 See, for example, Parsons (1974, 1992) on a more comprehenisve description of the Hawthorne experiments.

19 Roethlisberger and Dickson (1939, p.160) noted that "[the] efficacy of the wage incentive was so dependent on its relation to other factors that it was impossible to consider it in itself having an independent effect on the individual." Roethlisberger (1948, p.12-13) noted that "far from being the prime and sole mover of human activity in business, economic interest has run far behind in the list of incentives that make men willing to work ... man at work is a social creature as well as an economic man. He has personal and social as well as economic needs". While such an interpretation may go too far in discarding the motivational effect of monetary incentives, organizational behaviour theorists were induced by the Hawthorne experiments to look beyond monetary rewards when searching for a theory of motivation.

20 Some evidence on the retention argument is provided by the experience of UK Alliance and Leicester Building Society where employee turnover fell from 16 per cent to 11 per cent after a merit pay system was introduced in 1987. In addition, up to half of those employees which delivered sub-standard performance left the organisation until 1990 (IDS Top Pay Unit, 1990).

21 Negative effects on intrinsic motivation can only result, of course, when there is some degree of intrinsic motivation in the first place, i.e. when the job is in some way stimulating other needs than the sole strive for monetary rewards.

22 As Slater (1980, p.127) claims, for example, "using money as a motivator leads to a progressive degradation in the quality of everything produced".

23 Deci and Ryan (1985, p.49) observe that "intrinsic motivation is based in the need to be self-determining and ... rewards, which are widely used as in-struments of control, can often co-opt people's self-determination."

24 For empirical evidence on the introduction of pay for performance systems in the area of retail banking, see, for example, Goodswen (1988), Swabe (1989), and Otley (1992).

25 Tom Peters also favours team-based performance systems (1987, p. 337): "The team and the facility/division are the basic building blocks ... identification with these groups should be maximised, and the lion's share of variable compensation should follow from team/facility/division performance".

26 See, for example, Martin (1991) for a review of the organizational behaviour literature on working in groups.

Bancassurance in Europe: Conclusions and Suggestions for Further Research

This last part presents a brief summary of the main conclusions of the study and gives an outlook of the significance of cross-industry entry between banking and insurance in the future.

The first part of the study focused on the question why banks enter the insurance market, analysing industry- and firm-level incentives. It was noted that entry activities were in many ways a defensive move on the part of banks when starting around the mid-1980s. Insurance firms had progressively moved into traditional banking business, in particular in the life insurance sector where products constitute close substitutes to traditional banking products such as fund management, pension products and long-term savings plans. As banks were fearing further erosion of their retail deposit base, their most important source of funds for refinancing, a number of them decided to address insurer's inroads into banking business in an offensive way by extending their product portfolio to include life insurance products.

In addition to engaging in a purely defensive move, banks also perceived significant profit opportunities in life insurance. Demand for life insurance has been buoyant and growth rates significant over the past decade. This surge in demand stems at least partly from the fact that public pension systems do not provide the desired financial security and, as a result, consumers perceive an increased need to provide for private retirement planning, frequently encouraged by an advantageous tax regime for life insurance products. At the same time, banks' profit margins have been squeezed in many of their traditional activities resulting from increased competition in the deposits area as well as the wholesale loan sector where margins have been tumbling and there has been an increased need to provide substantial bad debt provisions due to a significant increase in loan defaults both in the retail as well as the corporate sector. Finally, banks increasingly perceive the need to optimally utilise their high fixed-cost retail branch network by including high-margin, low-risk life insurance in their product line at low marginal cost.

The changing regulatory environment concerning the entry of banks into insurance contributed to increased cross-industry penetration by facilitating entry. While regulators have for a long time enforced strict separation between the banking and insurance sectors, cross-industry entry has been facilitated recently by relaxing regulatory barriers. This liberalisation was at least partly caused by the insight that increased competition may entail substantial welfare benefits for consumers of financial services. Thus, while joint production of banking and insurance services continues to be prohibited in virtually all surveyed countries, de novo entry as well as cross-industry acquisitions and distribution agreements are now allowed in the majority of Western countries with the notable exceptions of Japan and the US.

Concerning firm-level incentives to enter the insurance market, this study focused on synergies between banking and insurance. Synergies exist if an integrated firm has a higher return on investment than a firm consisting of several stand-alone units. The two most important examples of cost synergies are economies of scale and scope. While scale economies do not appear significant in the context of bancassurance, scope economies provide a powerful explanation for banks' entry into insurance. They may result fom sharing common inputs, diversification advantages, marketing economies and lock-in effects of consumers resulting in switching costs.

Synergy effects are greater between banking and life insurance than for general insurance, as distribution costs constitute a much higher proportion of total costs in life insurance and therefore potential savings when utilising the branch network are more significant.

The second part of the study focused on the question how banks enter the insurance sector and identified the critical factors for success. I analysed thirteen case studies of entry strategies in order to compare the relative success of the four alternative entry options. As a result of this empirical analysis, it appears that de novo entry is the most successful entry route, since it allows a tailored and firm-specific entry strategy taking account of the idiosyncratic situation of the firm and its competitive environment. Costs of compromise are significantly greater for the other three entry vehicles. Mergers and acquisitions usually involve high adjustment costs, while strategic alliances and joint ventures are unlikely to be stable in the long term due to incentives for buying out the joint venture partner or terminating the alliance.

Further critical success factors for entry into insurance include an effective strategy of market segmentation which is critical for obtaining a competitive advantage. Market segmentation is required in order to adequately recognise customer needs and to create a strategic position which differentiates the supplier from its competitors. It also the basis of the distribution approach which is increasingly being fine-tuned according to the needs of different customer segments.

The traditionally different approaches with regard to compensation systems in banking and insurance present management with a decision problem whether to adopt a more performance-oriented pay structure or whether to maintain the traditional salary approach. Based on an analysis of the existing literature on pay for performance systems, I argued that a branch-based pay for performance system provides the best approach, as it encourages team work and avoids problems of introducing different payment systems side by side in the branch.

What are the conclusions of the study concerning the future outlook for bancassurance?

While just about half of the largest EC banks have so far expanded into the area of insurance, it is likely that those institutions which have not entered will do so in the future. This prediction is based on two arguments: firstly, those banks which have successfully entered insurance such as TSB and Credit Agricole are frequently cited as success stories, arousing interest among other European banks which are eager to emulate these entry moves. These examples have illustrated that a successful entry strategy offers significant profit potential for banks. Secondly, competitive pressures will be such that once other banks have entered insurance, those banks which have not done so are forced to emulate the moves of their competitors in order to prevent losing market share.

Bancassurance will therefore become an even more widely spread phenomenon. It is likely that most banks will internalise insurance activities which means that they either start out through a de novo entry in the first place or buy out co-operating partners. This move towards internalisation stems from the fact that in the long run, banks face the greatest profit potential when owning their own life insurance subsidiary.

For the area of general insurance the trend towards convergence is likely to be a lot slower, since synergies are significantly less than for life insurance. Nevertheless, at the end of this decade banks may offer the whole range of insurance services to their retail customers.

What are the limitations of the current research study and the chosen research approach and how can further research advance the state of know-how in the area of bancassurance? Furthermore, what degree of general applicability does the present study possess, i.e. to what group or type of institutions do the results of the study apply?

Firstly, the present research study focuses on a sample of the largest 60 banks in the European Community. Thus, it does not analyse the issue of bancassurance for the large number of medium-sized and smaller institutions. It may be the case that for these smaller institutions different criteria are important than for the large firms. For example, the choice of the entry vehicle may be influenced by company size. In order to test this hypothesis and to ascertain whether or not bank size has an influence on the strategic choices in the context of bancassurance, one could compare a sample of large institutions with a control sample of smaller firms and determine whether there are statistically significant differences in the characteristics and choices of the two sample groups.

Secondly, this study addressed the issue of bancassurance for four large EC countries, France, the UK, the Netherlands and Germany. It may now be interesting to analyse a sample of banks from other European countries in order to test whether the main conclusions of this study will be confirmed for a sample of institutions from these other countries. While this study showed that some of the key factors of success are identical for institutions across the four different countries which were analysed, it may still be the case that in other European countries these factors vary.

Thirdly, the research explored the strategic approach of a sample of institutions which had entered insurance. However, no comprehensive empirical evidence was collected on the sample of institutions which had *not* entered insurance. It may be interesting to further explore the reasons why these banks have - so far at least - decided not to enter insurance. Thus, a sample of institutions which have not entered insurance could be contacted and through interviews it may be possible to find out about the reasons why firms have not entered and in particular whether they plan to continue to abstain from this market or whether they intend to enter eventually.

Fourthly, the present study does not analyse the interaction between the banking and insurance industry in greater detail. In particular, it does not address the insurers' response to the inroads which banks are making into their traditional territory. Since insurers face inherent disadvantages, as their distribution channels are harder to adapt to banking products, it is likely that they will start to explore new distribution channels. These could consist, for example, of insurers acquiring banks, expanding their retail network or exploring new distribution channels such as telephone sales and direct marketing. Similarly, insurers could increasingly attempt to expand their product line to incorporate products which were traditionally only offered by banks. One can already observe some insurers which started to issue credit cards and even offer simple loan products in some countries. However, no empirical research exists to date analyse these developments. It would therefore be highly interesting to undertake a similar research study to the present one from the perspective of the insurance industry in order to analyse the actual or planned strategic response of insurers to the challenge posed by banks.[1] Such a study could consist, for example, of a similar set of case studies which analyse the strategic decisions of insurers which have responded to banks' entry into their traditional home turf.

Fifthly, the study employed the research methodology of a *multiple*-case study design, since this was considered to be most suitable for the research questions under scrutiny and it is the first study in the literature which has focused on the set of issues surrounding banks' entry into insurance using this method. Based on the results of this research study it would now be interesting to look at greater detail at some of the internal and organizational issues which arise in the context of introducing insurance products into a banking environment.

In particular, some of the issues surrounding the aspect of corporate culture deserve greater scrutiny, as it is not possible to glean a sufficiently clear picture of this issue from single interviews as carried out in this research study. This stems from the inherent limitations which the multiple case study method entails when the researcher remains an outsider to the organization and may therefore miss out on important issues which are not revealed to an outside observer.[2] It would therefore be highly elucidating to undertake a study which looks in greater depth at one or two selected institutions, employing a research approach of participant observation or action learning. Participant observation involves that the researcher spends an extended period of time in one organization up to a period of several months to get to know the internal structure and corporate culture of the institution (e.g. Moser and Kalton, 1979, p.249-254; Yin, 1989, p.92-94).[3] With action learning the researcher takes a more active role in the organization. Rather than just observing as a participant, the researcher is actively involved in the decision-making of the organization as a consultant and may even alter the course of events (Clark, 1972; Argyris *et al.*, 1986). These approaches have the advantage that the researcher has the opportunity "to look behind the scene" and gather a lot of information which may otherwise not be obtainable. As Whyte (1984, p.23) notes, "participant observation offers learning opportunities that cannot be duplicated by any other method".

In the context of bancassurance, participant observation or action learning promise to be the only research methods which can penetrate some of the most critical issues concerning the organizational and corporate culture aspects of integrating insurance products into the banking environment. In addition, an internal observer has the opportunity to gain first-hand experience concerning the implementation of an entry strategy into insurance. This includes potential problems and organizational resistance which may occur as part of this process about which organizations may be hesitant to talk about in personal interviews. Such a research approach could therefore provide valuable new insights and significantly carry forward the research area of bancassurance.

1 See, Aerthoj (1990) for some preliminary evidence.

2 See especially Gummesson (1988, chapter one) who discusses the important question of the researcher's access to the organization and of obtaining a sound and proper view of the organization.

3 Jorgensen (1989, p. 20-21) notes that "the participant role provides access to the world of everyday life from the standpoint of a member or insider ... it is a very special strategy and method for gaining access to the interior, seemingly subjective aspects of human existence".

Bibliography

Acheson, M. and Halstead, D. (1991), 'Trends in securitisation - private and public', in: D. Chew (ed.), *New Developments in Commercial Banking*, Oxford: Basil Blackwell

Adolf, R., Cramer, J. and Ollmann, M. (1991), 'Banking mergers: a realistic assessment of synergy effects', *Die Bank*, 1/91, 4-9

Aerthoj, O. (1990), 'The European insurance industry and the impact competition from banks will exert on it', in: D. Fair and C. de Boissieu (eds.), *Financial Institutions in Europe Under New Competitive Conditions*, Dordrecht: Kluwer Academic Publishers

Andersen, A. (1990), *Insurance in a Changing Europe*, 1990-95, London: The Economist Publications

Ansoff, I. (1965), *Corporate Strategy*, New York: John Wiley

Argyris, C., Putnam, R. and McLain Smith, D. (1986), *Action Science*, San Francisco: Jossey-Bass

Armstrong, M. and Murliss, H. (1991), *Reward Management*, London: Kogan Page

Arrow, K. (1962), 'The economic implications of learning by doing', *Review of Economic Studies*, **29**, 153-173

Artis, M. (1988), 'Exchange controls and the EMS', *European Economy*, **36**, 163-181

Athanasios, G., Subhash, C. and Miller, S. (1990), 'Returns to scale and input substitution for large U.S. Banks', *Journal of Money, Credit and Banking*, **22**, 94-107

Bagehot, W. (1873), *Lombard Street*, reprinted in 1962 by Richard D. Irwin, Illinois: Homewood

Bailey, E. and Friedlaender, A. (1982), 'Market structure and multiproduct industries', *Journal of Economic Literature*, **20**, 1024-1048

Balakrishnan, S. and Koza, M. (1989), 'Organisation costs and a theory of joint ventures', Working Paper, INSEAD

Baltensperger, E. and Dermine, J. (1992), 'European Banking: prudential and regulatory issues', in: *European Banking in the 1990's*, J. Dermine (ed.), Oxford: Basil Blackwell

Bank for International Settlements (1987), Committee on banking regulations and supervisory practise, *Proposals for international convergence of capital measurement and capital standards*, December

Barron, R. (1986), *Behaviour in Organizations*, Newton, MA: Allyn and Bacon

Baumol, W. (1977), 'On the proper cost tests for natural monopoly in a multiproduct industry', *American Economic Review*, **67**, 809-22

Baumol, W., Panzar, J. and Willig, R. (1982), *Contestable Markets and the Theory of Industry Structure*, New York: Harcourt Brace Jovanovich

Beamish, P. (1985), 'The characteristics of joint ventures in developed and developing countries', *Columbia Journal of World Business*, Winter, 13-19

Berger A., Hanweck, G. and Humphrey D. (1987), 'Competitive viability in banking: scale, scope and product mix economies', *Journal of Monetary Economics*, **20**, 501-520

Berger, A. and Humphrey. D. (1991), 'Measurement and efficiency issues in banking', in: *Output Measurement in the Services Sector*, NBER, Chicago: University of Chicago Press

Berlin, M., Saunders, A. and Udell, G. (1991), 'Deposit insurance reform: what are the issues and what needs to be fixed?', *Journal of Banking and Finance*, **15**, 735-752

Berry, L. (1980), 'Service marketing is different', *Business*, May/June

Berry, L., Parasuraman, A. and Zeithaml, V. (1992), 'Five imperatives for improving service quality' in: C. Lovelock (ed.), *Managing Services - Marketing, Operations and Human Resources*, Englewood Cliffs, NJ: Prentice Hall, reprinted from *Sloan Management Review*, **29**, 29-38

Boaden, R. and Dale, B. (1993), 'Managing quality improvements in financial services: a framework and case study', *Service Industries Journal*, **13**, 17-39

Boissieu, C. de (1990), 'Recent developments in the French financial system: an overview', in: C. de Boissieu, *Banking in France*, London: Routledge

Borden, N. (1965), 'The concept of the marketing mix', in: G. Schwartz (ed.), *Science in Marketing*, chapter 13, Wiley

Bowen, D. and Schneider, B. (1988), 'Services marketing and management: implications for organizational behaviour', *Research in Organizational Behaviour*, **10**, 43-80

Brady, L. and Wright, V. (1990), *Performance Related Pay*, Fact Sheet No.30, London: Personnel Management

Brittan, Sir Leon (1991), 'Financial Services and Financial Markets: a European Perspective', Speech held on 14 January 1991 before the American Chamber of Commerce, New York, mimeo, DG15, Commission of the EC

Brown, B. (1992), *Allfinanz without Limits - Learning from the TSB Experience*, London: Lafferty Publications

Bryan, L. (1991), 'Structured securitised credit: a superior technology for lending', in: D. Chew (ed.), *New Developments in Commercial Banking*, Oxford: Basil Blackwell

Buzzell, R. and Gale, B. (1992), 'Integrating strategies for clusters of business', in: K. Sommers Luchs and A. Campbell (eds.), *Strategic Synergy*, Oxford: Blackwells; originally published in 1987: *The PIMS Principles: Linking Strategy to Performance*, The Free Press

Cannel, M. and Wood, S. (1992), *Incentive Pay*, London: Institute for Personnel Management

Casson, M. (1990), 'Evolution of multinational banking: a theoretical perspective', in: *Banks as Multinationals*, G. Owen (ed.), London: Routledge

Caves, R. (1982), *Multinational Enterprise and Economic Analysis*, Cambridge: Cambridge University Press

Chandler, A. (1962), *Strategy and Structure: Chapters in the History of Industrial Enterprise*, Cambridge, MA: MIT Press

Chandler, A. (1982), 'The M-form: industrial groups, American style', *European Economic Review*, **19**, 3-23

Clark, P. (1972), *Action Research and Organizational Change*, London: Harper and Row

Clarke, C. and Brennan, K. (1990), 'Building Synergy in the Diversified Business', *Long-Range Planning*, **23**, 9-16

Coase, R. (1937), 'The nature of the firm', *Economica*, **4**, 386-405

Contractor, F. and Lorange, P. (1988), *Cooperative Strategies in International Business*, Lexington, MA: Lexington Books

Copeland, T. and Weston, F. (1988), *Financial Theory and Corporate Policy*, Reading, MA: Addison-Wesley

Cowell, D. (1984), *The Marketing of Services*, Oxford: Heinemann

Cowling, K. et al. (1980), *Mergers and Economic Performance*, Cambridge: Cambridge University Press

Darby, M. and Karny, E. (1973), 'Free competition and the optimal amount of fraud', *Journal of Law and Economics*, **16**, 67-88

Dasgupta, P. and Stiglitz, J. (1988), 'Learning-by-doing, market structure, and industrial and trade policies', *Oxford Economic Papers*, **40**, 246-68

Deci, E. and Ryan, R. (1985), *Intrinsic Motivation and Self-Dermination in Human Behaviour*, New York: Plenum Press

Dermine, J. and Röller, L. (1991), Economies of Scale and Scope in the French Mutual Funds (SICAV) industry, mimeo, Paris: INSEAD

Diamond, D. (1984), 'Financial intermediation and delegated monitoring', *Review of Economic Studies*, **55**, 377-90

Diamond, D. and Dybvig, P. (1983), 'Bank runs, deposit insurance and liquidity', *Journal of Political Economy*, **91**, 401-419

Dueser, J. (1990), *International Strategies of Japanese Banks: the European Perspective*, Basingstoke: Macmillan

Ennew, C., Wong, P. and Wright, M. (1992), 'Organisational structures and the boundaries of the firm: acquisitions and divestment in financial services', *Services Industries Journal*, **12**, 478-497

Ennew, C., Watkins, T. and Wright, M., (1990), *Marketing Financial Services*, Oxford: Heinemann

Ennew, C., Watkins, T. and Wright, M., (1993), 'Marketing financial services: an overview', in: Ennew, C., Watkins, T. and Wright, M. (eds.), *Cases in Marketing Financial Services*, Oxford: Heinemann Publishers

Eurostat (1992), *The Year in Figures*, Luxembourg: Office for Official Publications of the EC

Farrell, J. (1986), 'Moral hazard as an entry barrier', *Rand Journal of Economics*, **17**, 440-49

Fitchew, G. (1990), 'Overview: European financial markets - the Commission's proposals', in: *European Banking in the 1990's*, J. Dermine, ed. Oxford: Basil Blackwell

Fowler, F. and Mangione, T. (1990), *Standardized Survey Interviewing*, Applied Social Research Methods Series, Vol. 18, Newbury Park: Sage Publications

Fudenberg, D. and Tirole, J. (1983), 'Learning by doing and market performance', *Bell Journal of Economics*, **14**, 522-530

Gapper, J. (1993), 'Nat West seeks a new life', *Financial Times*, 5 January 1993

Gapper, J. (1993b), 'For richer, not poorer', *Financial Times*, 14 May 1993

Gapper, J. (1993c) 'Banks launch root and branch reform', *Financial Times*, 8 January 1993

Gardener, E. (1990), 'European Financial Supermarkets?', Research Papers in Banking and Finance, Institute of European Finance, University College of North Wales, Bangor

Gardener, E. (1991), 'Strategic Developments in European Banking', Research Papers in Banking and Finance, Institute of European Finance, University College of North Wales, Bangor

Gardener, E. (1992), 'Capital adequacy and its impact on banks and regulators', in: *New Issues in Financial Services*, R. Kinsella (ed.), Oxford: Blackwell Publisher

Gardener, E. (1992b), 'Banking strategies and 1992', in: A. Mullineaux (ed.), *European Banking*, Oxford: Basil Blackwell

Gardener, E. and Molyneux, P. (1990), *Changes in Western European Banking*, London: Unwin Hyman

George, W. and Myers, T. (1981), 'Life underwriters' perceptions of differences in selling goods and services', *CLU Journal*, April, 44-49

Gilligan, T. and Smirlock, M. (1984), 'An empirical study of joint production and scale economies in commercial banking', *Journal of Banking and Finance*, 8, 67-76

Glaser, B. and Strauss, A. (1967), *The Discovery of Grounded Theory*, Chicago: Aldine

Goodhart, C. (1989), *Money, Information and Uncertainty*, London: Macmillan

Goodswen, M. (1988), 'Retention and reward of the high achiever', *Personnel Management*, October

Grant, R. (1992), 'Diversification in the financial services industry', in: K. Sommers Luchs and A. Campbell (eds.), *Strategic Synergy*, Oxford: Blackwells

Gummesson, E. (1988), *Qualitative Methods in Management Research*, Bromwell: Chartwell-Bratt

Harrigan, K. (1986), *Managing for Joint Venture Success*, Lexington, MA: Lexington

Hawawini, G. and Rajera, E. (1990), 'The transformation of the European financial services industry: from fragmentation to integration', Working Paper, Paris: INSEAD

Hopkins, B. (1992), 'Introduction', in: *Pay for Performance, History, Controversy, and Evidence*, B. Hopkins and T. Mawhinney (eds.), New York: Haworth Press

Howcroft, B. (1991), 'Customer satisfaction in retail banking', *Service Industries Journal*, **11**, 11-17

Hughes, A. (1989), 'The impact of merger: a survey of empirical evidence for the UK', in: J. Fairburn and J. Kay (eds.), *Mergers and Merger Policy*, Oxford: Oxford University Press

Humphrey, T. (1989), 'Lender of last resort: The concept in history', *Economic Review*, Federal Reserve Bank of Richmond, March/April, 8-16

Hunter, W., Timme, S. and Yang, W. (1990), 'An examination of cost subadditivity and multiproduct production in large U.S. banks', *Journal of Money, Credit and Banking*, **22**, 504-525

IDS Top Pay Unit (1990), Review 110

Imfeld, D. (1991), 'Economies of scale in the insurance industry', Swiss Reinsurance Company, *Sigma*, 4/91

Itami, H. (1992), 'Invisible assets', in: K. Sommers Luchs and A. Campbell (eds.), *Strategic Synergy*, Oxford: Blackwells; originally published in 1987 as *Mobilising Invisible Assets*, Cambridge, MA: Harvard University Press

Jacklin, C. (1987), 'Banks and risk sharing: instabilities and coordination', in: S. Bhattacharya and N. Wallace (eds.), *Financial Markets and Incomplete Information*, Rowman & Littlefield Publishers

Jacklin, C. (1990), 'Demand equity and deposit insurance', Research Paper No.1062, Graduate School of Business, Stanford University

Jacklin, C. and Bhattachrya, S. (1988), 'Distinguishing panics and information-based bank runs', *Journal of Political Economy*, **96**, 568-592

Jacobs, A (1993), 'ING Group: from strategy to reality', paper presented at EFMA Congress, Monaco, 17 March 1993

Jorgensen, D. (1989), *Participant Observation*, Beverly Hills: Sage Publications

Kane, E. (1989), 'The high cost of incompletely funding the FSLIC's shortage of explicit capital', *Journal of Economic Perspectives*, **3**, 31-47

Kanfer, R. (1990), 'Motivation Theory and Industrial and Organizational Psychology', in: *Handbook of Industrial and Organizational Psychology*, M. Dunnette and L. Hough (eds.), Palo Alto, CA: Consulting Psychologists Press

Kareken, J. and Wallace N. (1978), 'Deposit insurance and bank regulation: a partial equilibrium exposition', *Journal of Business*, **51**, 413-438

Katzenbach, J. and Smith, D. (1992), 'Why teams matter', *McKinsey Quarterly*, **3**, 3-27

Katzenbach, J. and Smith, D. (1993), The Wisdom of Teams: *Creating the High-Performance Organization*, Boston, MA: Harvard Busniess School Press

Kaufman, G. (1988), 'The truth about bank runs', in: C. England and T. Huertas (eds.), *The Financial Services Revolution*, Boston: Kluwer Academic Publishers

Klein, B., Crawford, R. and Alchian, A. (1978), 'Vertical integration, appropriable rents, and the competitive contracting process', *Journal of Law and Economics*, **21**, 297-326

Klemperer, P. (1987a), 'Entry deterrence in markets with consumer switching costs', *Economic Journal*, **97**, 99-117

Klemperer, P. (1987b), 'Markets with consumer switching costs', *Quarterly Journal of Economics*,

Klemperer, P. (1989), 'Price wars caused by switching costs', Discussion Paper No. 40, Oxford: Nuffield College

Klemperer, P. (1990), 'Product line competition and shopping costs: why firms may choose to compete head-to-head', Discussion Paper No.55, Oxford: Nuffield College

Kim, H. (1986), 'Economies of scale and economies of scope in multiproduct financial institutions: further evidence from credit unions', *Journal of Money, Credit and Banking*, **18**, 220-226

Kindleberger, C. (1978), *Manias, Panics and Crashes: A History of Financial Crises*, New York: Basic Books

Kogut, B. (1989a), 'Joint ventures: theoretical and empirical perspectives', *Strategic Management Journal*, 9, 319-32

Kogut, B. (1989b), 'The stability of joint ventures: reciprocity and competitive rivalry', *Journal of Industrial Economics*, 28, 183-198

Kopper, H. (1990), 'Strategische Ausrichtunng einer Universalbank auf einen gemeinsamen EG-Finanzmarkt', *Österreichisches Bankarchiv*, 2/90

Korf, U. and Dorner, M. (1991), 'Allfinanz durch Kooperation', *Bank und Markt*, June 1991

Kotler, P. (1991), *Marketing Management: Analysis, Planning, Implementation and Control*, New York: Prentice Hall

Kreps, D. (1990), 'Corporate culture and economic theory' in: J. Alte and K. Shepsle (eds.), *Rational Perspectives on Positive Political Economy*, Cambridge: Cambridge University Press

Lafferty Publications (1990), *The Allfinanz Revolution*, London: Lafferty Publications

Lane, D. (1991), 'Banks in Italy: Much ado about something', *The Banker*, August

Lechner, R. and Enz, R. (1993), 'Assekuranz Global 1991: Neuer Aufschwung in Europa - Stagnation und Rückgang in Asien und Nordamerika', *Sigma*, 4/93

Lebegue, D. (1993), 'Une demache legitime', *La Tribune de L'Assurance*, La Tribune Desfosses, p.23

Lepper, M., Greene, D. and Nisbett, R. (1973), 'Undermining children's intrinsic interest with extrinsic reward: A test of the overjustification hypothesis', *Journal of Personality and Social Psychology*, **28**, 129-137

Lepper, M. and Greene, D. (1978), *The Hidden Costs of Rewards: New Perspectives on the Psychology of Human Motivation*, Hillsdale, NJ: Lawrence Applebaum

Levitt, T. (1960), 'Marketing myopia', *Harvard Business Review*, July/August, 45-56

Levitt, T. (1975), 'Marketing Myopia', *Harvard Business Review*, September/October,

Llewellyn, D. (1990), 'Competition, diversification and structural change in the British financial system', in: D. Fair and C. de Boissieu (eds.), *Financial Institutions in Europe Under New Competitive Conditions*, Dordrecht: Kluwer Academic Publishers

Löhneysen, E., Viana, A. and Walton, A., (1990), 'Emerging roles in European retail banking', *McKinsey Quarterly*, 3, 127-35

Lorange, P. and Roos, J. (1992), *Strategic Alliances - Formation, Implementation and Evolution*, Oxford: Blackwell

Lovelock, C. (1983), 'Classifying services to gain strategic marketing insights', *Journal of Marketing*, **47**, 9-20

Lovelock, C. (1992), 'Are services really different?' in: C. Lovelock (ed.), *Managing Services - Marketing, Operations and Human Resources*, Englewood Cliffs, NJ: Prentice Hall

Lovelock, (1992b), 'Designing and managing the customer-service function', in: C. Lovelock (ed.), *Managing Services - Marketing, Operations and Human Resources*, Englewood Cliffs, NJ: Prentice Hall

Mariti, P. and Smiley, R. (1983), 'Cooperative agreements and the organisation of industry', *Journal of Industrial Economics*, **31**, 437-451

Markowitz, H. (1959), Portfolio Selection: Efficient Diversification of Investments, New York: Wiley

Martin, R. (1991), 'Working in Groups', in: M. Smith (ed.), *Analysing Organizational Behaviour*, London: Macmillan

Martin, S. (1992), 'Mergers and economic performance', Working Paper, Department of Economics, European University Institute, Florence, Italy

Maskin, E. and Riley, J. (1985), 'Auction theory with private values', *American Economic Review*, Papers and Proceedings, **75**, 150-155

Maslow, A. (1943), 'A theory of human motivation', *Psychological Review*, **50**, 370-96

Mawhinney, T., Dickinson, A. and Taylor, L. (1989), 'The use of concurrent schedules to evaluate the effects of extrinsic rewards on intrinsic motivation', *Journal of Organisational Behaviour Management*, **8**, 89-105

Mayer, C. (1992), 'The regulation of financial services: lessons from the United Kingdom for 1992', in: *European Banking in the 1990's*, J. Dermine, ed., Oxford: Basil Blackwell

McCarthy, E. (1981), *Basic Marketing: A Managerial Approach*, Homewood, IL: Richard D. Erwin

McDowell, B. (1989), *Deregulation and Competition in the Insurance Industry*, New York: Quorum Books

Meeks, G. (1977), *Disappointing Marriage: A Study of the Gains from Merger*, Cambridge: Cambridge University Press

Merrick, D. and Saunders, A. (1985), 'Bank regulation and monetary policy', *Journal of Money, Credit and Banking*, **17**, 691-717

Mester, L. (1987), 'A multiproduct cost study of Savings and Loan Associations', *Journal of Finance*, **42**, 423-445

Milgrom, P. (1987), 'Auction Theory', in: *Advances in Economic Theory*, T. Bewley (ed.), Cambridge: Cambridge University Press

Mintzberg, H. (1983), 'An emerging strategy of direct research in qualitative methodology" in: *Qualitative Methodology*, J. Van Maanen (ed.)

Mintzberg, H., Quinn, J. and James, R. (1988), *The Strategy Process-Concepts, Contexts and Cases*, Englewood Cliffs, NJ: Prentice-Hall

Mitchell, T. (1982), 'Motivation: new directions for theory, research and practice, *Academy of Management Review*, **7**, 80-88

Moser, C. and Kalton, G. (1979), *Survey Methods in Social Investigation*, Hants: Gower

Moss Kanter, R. (1989), *When Giants Learn To Dance*, London: Simon and Schuster

Mueller, D. (1989), 'Mergers - causes, effects and policies', *International Journal of Industrial Organisation*, **7**, 1-10

Murray, J. and White, R. (1983), 'Economies of scale and economies of scope in multiproduct financial institutions: a study of British Columbia credit unions, *Journal of Finance*, **38**, 887-902

Nelson, P. (1970), 'Information and consumer behaviour', *Journal of Political Economy*, **78**, 311-29

Neven, D. (1985), 'Two-stage (perfect) equilibrium in Hotelling's model', *Journal of Industrial Economics*, **33**, 317-325

Neven, D. (1992), 'Structural adjustment in European retail banking: some views from industrial organisation', in: J. Dermine (ed.), *European Banking in the 1990's*, Oxford: Basil Blackwell

OECD (1989), *Competition in Banking*, Paris: OECD Publications

OECD (1992), *Insurance and other Financial Services: Structural Trends*, Paris: OECD Publications

OECD (1992b), *Bank Profitability: Statistical Supplements*, Paris: OECD Publications

Otley, D. (1992), 'United Bank: a case study on the implementation of a performance-related reward scheme', in: W. Burus (ed.), *Performance Measurements, Evaluation and Incentives*, Boston, MA: Harvard Business School Press

Padoa-Schioppa (1987), *Efficiency, Stability and Equity*, Oxford: Oxford University Press

Panzar, J. and Willig, R. (1977), 'Economies of scale in multi-output production', *Quarterly Journal of Economics*, **91**, 431-93

Panzar, J. and Willig, R. (1981), 'Economies of Scope', *American Economic Review*, **71**, 268-272

Parsons, H. (1974), 'What happened at Hawthorne?, *Science*, **183**, 922-32

Parsons, H. (1992), 'Hawthorne: an early OBM experiment', in: *Pay for Performance, History, Controversy, and Evidence*, B. Hopkins and T. Mawhinney (eds.), New York: Haworth Press

Pauluhn, B. (1991), 'Everything from one source - a strategy for the future', *Bank und Markt*, June 1991

Peach, E. and Wren, D. (1992), 'Pay for performance from antiquity to the 1950s', in: *Pay for Performance, History, Controversy, and Evidence*, B. Hopkins and T. Mawhinney (eds.), New York: Haworth Press

Penrose, E. (1959), *Theory of the Growth of the Firm*, Oxford: Basil Blackwell

Peters, T. (1987), *Thriving on Chaos*, New York: Alfred A. Knopf

Porter, M. (1980), *Competitive Strategy: Techniques for Analysing Industries and Competitors*, New York: The Free Press

Porter, M. (1985), *Competitive Advantage: Creating and Sustaining Superior Performance*, New York: The Free Press

Porter, L. and Lawler, E. (1968), 'What job attitudes tell about motivation', *Harvard Business Review*, **46**, 118-26

Postlewaite, A. and Vives, X. (1987), 'Bank runs as an equilibrium phenomenon', *Journal of Political Economy*, **95**, 485-491

Potvliege, F. *et al.* (1992), Convergence of Banking and Insurance: Current Thinking and Practice, Paper presented at European Banking and Securities Conference, McKinsey&Company, Barcelona

Prahalad, C. and Doz, Y. (1992), 'Evaluating interdependencies across businesses' in: K. Sommers Luchs and A. Campbell (eds.), *Strategic Synergy*, Oxford: Blackwells; originally published in 1986 in*The Multinational Mission: Balancing Local Demands and Global Vision*, The Free Press

Prosperetti, L. (1991), 'Economies of scale in Italian life-insurance', *Geneva Papers on Risk and Insurance*, **16**, 282-292

Ravenscraft, D. and Scherer, F. (1987), *Mergers, Sell-Offs, amd Economic Efficiency*, Washington, D.C.: Brookings Institution

Ravenscraft, D. and Scherer, F. (1989), 'The profitability of mergers', *International Journal of Industrial Organisation*, **7**, 101-116

Reichheld, F. and Sasser, W. (1990), 'Zero defections: quality comes to services', *Harvard Business Review*, September/October

Revell, J. (1991), 'Changes in Universal Banks and the Effect on Bank Mergers', Research Papers in Banking and Finance, Institute of European Finance, University College of North Wales, Bangor

Reynolds, R. and Snapp, B. (1986), 'The competitive effects of partial equity interests and joint ventures', *International Journal of Industrial Organisaztion*, 4, 141-153

Rodriguez, J. *et al.* (1993), 'Scale and Scope Economies in Banking: a study of Savings Banks in Spain', Research Papers in Banking and Finance, Institute of European Finance, University College of North Wales, Bangor

Roethlisberger, F. and Dickson, W. (1939), *Management and the Worker*, Cambridge, MA: Harvard University Press

Roethlisberger, F. (1948), 'A new look for management', in: *Worker Morale and Productivity*, New York: American Management Association

Salomon Brothers (1990), The Evolution of a Single European Banking Market, London: Salomon Brothers Research

Schien, E. (1985), *Organizational Culture and Leadership*, San Francisco: Jossey Base

Schneider, B. (1988), 'Notes on climate and culture', in: C. Lovelock (ed.), *Managing Services - Marketing, Operations and Human Resources*, first edition, Englewood Cliffs, NJ: Prentice Hall

Shaked, A. and Sutton, J. (1982), 'Relaxing price competition through product differentiation', *Review of Economic Studies*, **49**, 3-14

Shapiro, C. (1983), 'Optimal pricing of experience goods', *Bell Journal of Economics*, **14**, 497-507

Sharpe, S. (1990), 'Asymmetric information, bank lending and implicit contracts: a stylised model of customer relationships', *Journal of Finance*, **45**, 1069-87

Shostak, G. (1982), 'How to design a service', *European Journal of Marketing*, **16**, 49-63

Smith, W. (1956), 'Product differentiation and market segmentation as alternative marketing strategies', *Journal of Marketing*, July, 3-8

Smith, I. (1989), *People and Profits*, London: Croner

Speed, R. and Smith, G. (1992), 'Retail financial services segmentation', *Services Industries Journal*, **12**, 368-83

Spence, M. (1981), 'The learning curve and competition', *Bell Journal of Economics*, **12**, 49-70

Steinherr, A. and Gilibert, P. (1989), *The Impact of Financial Market Integration on the European Banking Industry*,

Brussels: Centre for European Policy Studies, Research Report No. 1

Stokey, N. (1986), 'The dynamics of industry-wide learning', in: W. Heller, R. Starr and D. Starrett (eds.), *Equilibrium Ananlysis: Essays in Honour of Kenneth J. Arrow*, Cambridge: Cambridge University Press

Swabe, A. (1989), 'Performance-related pay: a case study', *Employer Relations*, **11**, 17-22

Taylor, F. (1903), Shop management, New York: Harper & Row

Taylor, F. (1911), The principles of scientific management, New York: Harper & Row

Thierry, H. (1987), 'Payment by results systems: a review of research 1945-85', *Applied Psychology: An international review*, **36**, 1, 91-108

Vives, X. (1991), 'Banking competition and European integration', in: A. Giovannini and C. Mayer (eds.), *European Financial Integration*, Cambridge: Cambridge University Press

Vroom, V. (1964), *Work and Motivation*, New York: Wiley

Weizsäcker, C.-C. von (1984), 'The costs of substitution', *Econometrica*, **52**, 1085-1116

Weiner, B. (1980), *Human Motivation*, New York: Holt, Rinehart and Winston

White, L. (1989), 'The reform of federal deposit insurance', *Journal of Economic Perspectives*, **3**, 11-29

Whyte, W. (1984), *Learning from the Field*, Beverly Hills: Sage Publications

Williams (1920), *What's on the Worker's Mind? By One Who Put On Overalls to Find Out*, New York: Charles Scribner's Sons

Williamson, O. (1975), *Markets and Hierarchies: Analysis and Anti-Trust Implications*, New York: The Free Press

Williamson, O. (1989), 'Transcation cost economics', in: R. Schmalensee and R. Willig (eds.), *Handbook of Industrial Organisation*, Vol.1, Elsevier Science Publishers B.V.

Wright, P. (1987), 'Motivation and job satisfaction', in C. Molander (ed.), *Personnel Management: a Practical Introduction*, 65-83, Bromley, Kent: Chartwell Bratt

Yin, R. (1989), *Case Study Research*, Applied Social Research Methods Series, Vol.5, Newbury Park: Sage Publications

Zaniecki (1935), *The Method of Sociology*, New York: Holt, Rhinehart and Whinston

Zaniecki (1965), *Social Relations and Social Roles*, San Francisco: Chandler

Index